Szatmár Story

*A Family Narrative from the Shoah, with
Some Reflections On Its Meaning*

JEAN AXELRAD CAHAN

Archway Publishing books may be ordered through booksellers or by contacting:

Archway Publishing
1663 Liberty Drive
Bloomington, IN 47403
www.archwaypublishing.com
844-669-3957

Scripture taken from The Holy Scriptures © Koren Publishers Jerusalem Ltd., Jerusalem/Israel 1992.

ISBN: 978-1-6657-1533-1 (sc)
ISBN: 978-1-6657-1534-8 (e)

Library of Congress Control Number: 2021923404

Print information available on the last page.

Archway Publishing rev. date: 12/14/2021

To the memory of the two families described here,
and to Lara and Svea.

*For my father and my mother have forsaken
me, but the Lord will take me up.*
(Psalm 27:10)

And so long as you say 'one' instead of 'I,' there's nothing in it and one can easily tell the story; but as soon as you admit to yourself that it is you yourself, you feel as though transfixed and horrified. (Kafka, Wedding Preparations in the Country)

Contents

Acknowledgements.. xi
Preface xiii

I Narrative... 1
Father.. 1
Czernowitz and Vienna: Father's Early Years........................ 1
The Rise of Austro-Fascism... 5
The Anschluss-- Family Departure.. 9
First Years in Szatmárnémeti... 13
Hungary, the Eastern Front, and the Labor Service System...... 18
Death Marches: Budapest- Nagy-Czenk (Gross-
Zinkendorf)-Mauthausen.. 27
Gunskirchen 34
Mother.. 39
Szatmárnémeti Before the War 39
German Invasion of Hungary and Planning for Jewish
Destruction 46
The Fekete Family 1942-1944... 52
Ghettoization and Deportation 59
Auschwitz and Zittau.. 65
Afterwards 69
Budapest-Sydney-Montreal 69
Conclusion... 79

II Essay: Does the Holocaust Have Any Meaning? Jewish
Thought After the Holocaust..83
    Introduction...83
    The Holocaust in Hungary...85
    Did Transylvania Have a Special Role During the Hitler Era?...93
    Are There Political Lessons from the Holocaust Overall?...........96
    On Writing Jewish History 101
    Does the Holocaust Have a Religious Meaning?.....................102
    Exodus Politics?...117

About the Author...127

Acknowledgements

Apart from my immediate family, Catherine Chatterley, director of the Canadian Institute for the Study of Antisemitism, was the first to offer support and constructive commentary on this project. Alvin Rosenfeld, director of the Institute for the Study of Contemporary Antisemitism at Indiana University, similarly provided careful reading of an earlier draft and helpful advice.

I am most grateful to the Norman and Bernice Harris Center for Judaic Studies at the University of Nebraska-Lincoln for research support in various forms over several years. I especially appreciate the generous support, both financial and intellectual, by the Center's current director, Ariel Kohen, in the closing stages of writing and manuscript preparation. Two colleagues and friends at UNL, Bedross Der Matossian and Albert Casullo, a historian and a philosopher respectively, read drafts with great sensitivity and provided thoughtful comments. Former Dean of the College of Arts and Sciences Joseph S. Francisco also gave valuable support, without which this book either would not have been written or would have appeared many years later.

Two people with connections to Hungary and to Szatmár were enormously helpful: Katalin Petroczy provided excellent and efficient translation services, and Gyuri Elefant's website and ebook about Szatmár before, during and after the Shoah proved invaluable. Mr. Elefant was also extremely helpful in correspondence.

I would like to express my profound and loving gratitude to my husband, David, for a lifetime of intellectual companionship, for walking the "Spanish Steps" at Mauthausen with me, and for always (literally and figuratively) having a steadying hand under my elbow. His very sharp humor continues to have a beneficial, deflationary effect on my more mystical tendencies.

Lincoln, Nebraska

August 2021

Preface

The name 'Szatmár' evokes various thoughts and feelings in various audiences.[1] Within the Jewish world, it evokes either a certain awe and reverence for a strict, ultra-Orthodox religious community, or it inspires contempt mixed with a tincture of horror. To the outside world, it is simply a dilapidated, uninteresting town in the quasi-fictional territory of Transylvania. To me, it is the point of convergence of my parents' lives, perhaps unusual not only within the terms of the *univers concentrationnaire* established by the Nazis, but extraordinary in the resilience shown in the aftermath. Hence the title of this memoir.

My father transmitted only the barest outline of his life before and during the *Shoah*. It was an austerity probably born of several causes, including the customary reticence of men of that generation, and of men who have seen the worst of warfare, as well as a deep reluctance to call up memories of a destroyed family, and thereby to undermine one's capacity to go on living. He did once

---

[1] 'Szatmár' is the short form and most common manner of referring to the town of Szatmárnémeti among Hungarian-language speakers, among whom my mother grew up. After many conflicts, the city today lies within Romanian jurisdiction and is labelled on maps as 'Satu Mare,' the Romanian-language version of the name. The name of the famous Hasidic sect 'Satmar' is thus neither Hungarian nor Romanian, but most likely Yiddish in origin. (Thus the explanation for the sect's name given by Deborah Feldman, in her recent bestselling autobiography, *Unorthodox,* is incorrect.)

or twice (literally) mention that immediately after his release from Mauthausen, he was laid up, perhaps even hospitalized, with severe depression. But in this instance, as in many others, the details were extremely vague. While I learned more about my mother's experiences, she tended toward impressionistic accounts which, while powerful and conveying basic truths, were accompanied by limited knowledge of various other aspects of the war and persecution.

Though my parents spoke little about the Holocaust both before I became an adult and after, I knew without knowing, so to speak. This is difficult to explain. There were indicators along the way, both very large and very subtle. First of all, I had no grandparents, aunts and uncles, or cousins, and was therefore not able to chat, joke or complain casually with other children about my various relatives. Second, occasionally a phrase would fall: "the war," "at home [meaning pre-war Europe]," "my sister Emmy was very particular about her clothes [said while polishing shoes]." The world of yesterday was ever-present, though it did not prevent us from getting on with contemporary everyday life. It was only at the age of eighteen, quite unexpectedly, that I learned some details about my mother's experiences. After that occasion, both parents were slightly more inclined to mention the past openly, but overall they remained highly reticent. My mother and I were cross-country skiing in the Laurentian Mountains about an hour north of Montreal. It was an exceptionally beautiful spring day, with the sun glistening on fresh powdery snow sprinkled through the woods, and a brilliant blue sky. For whatever reason, perhaps because she was reminded of ski trips in the Carpathians during her youth, my mother stopped and, leaning against a thick tree branch which had bent over, started to talk.

Though she gave me a broad sketch, interspersed with a few details such as the *Appell* routine at Auschwitz, I never received any sort of day-today or even year-by-year account. This memoir therefore relies to a considerable extent on the work of historians, which has enabled me to partially reconstruct the events and processes my parents lived through. Whatever the divergences between historians on any given topic, and especially the Holocaust (for example, as between intentionalists and functionalists), I take historical reconstruction in this case to be a relatively uncomplicated process. I will therefore not have anything to say about methodological issues. The relationship between memory and history, for my purpose here, is simply one of reciprocity: history clarifies, explains, and illuminates the bare circumstances reported orally by those who lived through them; the information, both verbal and non-verbal, conveyed by the survivors, in turn makes more immediate and intense the events recounted by historians with no personal connection to the topic at hand. I do not believe that any conflict between memory and history arises in the story presented here. My parents made no specific claims which could be disconfirmed by historical research. They provided only a very broad outline of their itineraries, so to speak, and the merest hints as to their emotional responses, on which they alone would be expert. Their presence in various camps and their material losses were confirmed through the process of applying for reparations from the German government and by the International Tracing Service.

The historical work has shown me even more forcefully how discreet and austere my parents were in their revelations: the horrors they experienced were barely mentioned, let alone described, and the fact of their survival, especially in my father's case, was extraordinary. Nonetheless, the narrative presented here necessarily remains a form of collage or montage, a juxtaposition of large historical and geographical fragments, with smaller interpolations from my parents' memories as well as excerpts from my maternal grandfather's contemporaneous letters.

One of the conclusions I have come to is that remembering and memorializing are forms not only of love, but of justice. That is the wellspring of my motivation to write. In times when it was still common to believe that everyone would be rewarded or punished in another world beyond the grave, or at least, as Spinoza put it, that the idea of every individual would remain in the mind of God, the task of remembering was perhaps less onerous. But nowadays, when it seems that only human memory serves the dead, recording the history of unnaturally abbreviated lives, and horrors inflicted on innocent selves, appears to be the only form of rectification of inexpressible injustice, reparations payments and trials of war criminals notwithstanding. The publication of narratives about individual lives and deaths during the Holocaust is, as Ruth Wisse has perspicaciously put it, a means of "[undoing] the leveling work of the Nazi regime," that is, a means of undoing the erasure of individuality in the program of mass deportation and death.[2] A further, perhaps more mundane consideration in undertaking this memoir is the fact that, compared to the Holocaust in Poland and Germany, the Hungarian and Trans-Danubian context seems to be less well-known, even though studies of the Holocaust in the "borderlands" of Eastern Europe have recently increased considerably.[3]

To my sorrow, I have arrived at another conclusion. The metaphor of departure, journeying, and arrival is indeed apposite here. For I started out, as a teenager who encountered the works of Spinoza on my parents' bookshelf in Montreal, on a lifelong exploration of (what I only later came to understand as) the question of "how is Judaism still possible?" For me this was always predominantly a religious and philosophical question, though for others it took other forms. I would have loved to find evidence that the Orthodox Jews

---

[2] Ruth Wisse, "Introduction," in Robert Moses Shapiro (ed.), *Holocaust Chronicles: Individualizing the Holocaust through Diaries and Other Contemporaneous Personal Accounts* (Hoboken, NJ: Ktav Publishing House Inc., 1999), xviii.

[3] See for example: Alexander V. Prusin, *The Lands Between: Conflict in the East European Borderlands, 1870-1992* (Oxford: Oxford University Press, 2010); Timothy Snyder, *Bloodlands: Europe Between Hitler and Stalin* (New York: Basic Books, 2010).

of Szatmár, better than anyone else, understood the religious and moral secrets of the universe, and that their ways and traditions would solve the questions, for Jews, both of meaning and of how to live. That turned out to be far from where I landed. Whatever truth and beauty remain enveloped in the depths of their religious ideas, it is not enough to render a religious meaning to, let alone justify, the suffering that took place during the Shoah, and it did not enable the Orthodox of Szatmár to conduct themselves any more ethically than anyone else during that time. Perhaps not less ethically, but not more. If there is any lesson regarding this suffering, then it is a political one: centuries of dehumanizing language, racial and religious prejudice, social and legal discrimination, all ceaselessly watering the societal ground, create the conditions which permit violence and genocide to emerge and grow. States, constitutions and governments can either help or hinder these processes, they are the framework within which everything else takes place. Thus the answer to the question of how to understand the Holocaust lies, I believe, more in politics than in religion. So this is, in effect, my own theologico-political treatise. [4]

From Spinoza and Locke in the seventeenth century to Rawls in the twentieth, the liberal idea of a modern state and its distribution of goods, material, intellectual and spiritual, was an ideal for many in the West. What we observe in the first half of the twentieth century in Europe, however, was the complete failure of states to provide a framework of social, inter-ethnic and inter-religious peace and stability; on the contrary, instability was often expressly stoked up by governments. There are a great many reasons for these political choices, and it is beyond the scope of the present memoir to study them. I will only mention those that I think are relevant to my parents' story.

Within Jewish history and culture, philosophy has often served

---

[4] A reference to the classic work (1670) by Baruch Spinoza.

as a vital source of religious support, if not motivation. Many figures, from the Egyptian Philo of Alexandria (c.20 BCE-c.50 CE), through Maimonides and the Neo-Platonists (such as the Portugese Leon Ebreo (1464-1530) and Bahya Ibn Pakuda (1050-1120), from Al-Andalus), down to the German thinkers Hermann Cohen (1842-1918) and Franz Rosenzweig (1886-1929), contributed to what might be called the philosophico-religious tradition. After Auschwitz, as Theodor Adorno famously remarked, not only poetry but philosophy became impossible. In face of the historical facts, it was not merely indecent to pursue purely abstract, intellectual activities, but whatever concepts could be dreamed up would be totally inadequate to explain what had happened or to propose a program for the future. In other words, whatever role had been played by philosophy in the theophanic space[5], and indeed theology itself, was now shaken to its foundations. Nonetheless, numerous postwar thinkers, including Hans Jonas, Arthur Cohen, Emil Fackenheim and Emmanuel Levinas, attempted to "reboot" Jewish philosophy and a philosophical conception of God. Apart from the conceptual difficulties intrinsic to such endeavours, as Steven Katz has argued they are at a very far remove from traditional Jewish religious conceptions, and as such unconvincing.[6] These are the problems which have run like a red kabbalistic thread through my own life.

Even though this has been my central preoccupation, I will not be entering here at book length into what, if anything, philosophy can still contribute to the great questions of Jewish thought and identity after the Holocaust. It would take us too far afield, into questions about the recently-developed primacy of ethics

---

[5] I borrow this phrase from Peter Sloterdijk, *Not Saved: Essays After Heidegger* (Cambridge: Polity Books, 2016).

[6] Steven T. Katz, Shlomo Biderman, Gershon Greenberg (eds.), *Wrestling with God: Jewish Theological Responses after the Holocaust* (Oxford: Oxford University Press,2007), 620.

over metaphysics, the role of pragmatism, and many other quite esoteric matters. However, since I do see religion in some form as still central to Jewish identity, in Part II of this text I shall engage to some extent with the theological perspectives adopted by three prominent Hungarian-Transylvanian thinkers who arose in the same historical context as my parents: Yoel Teitelbaum, Eliezer Berkovits and Elie Wiesel. Even a relatively brief consideration of their responses to the Holocaust will reveal the enormity of the conceptual challenges facing Jewish philosophy and theology in the postwar era.

To the reader, the text presented here may appear as a strange combination of memoir-set-in historical context- plus limited philosophical reflections (not a full-blown theodicy or theology). I can hear unspoken thoughts: what's the matter with her, doesn't she have a neurosis or a syndrome to discuss, like other children of survivors? Although neither I nor my parents were aware of it, while I was in high school in Montreal in the mid- nineteen sixties, innovative investigations were begun by Dr. Vivian Rakoff, a researcher at the Jewish General Hospital there, on severe psychological disturbances in many of the "second generation." Reading about these studies many years later, I saw that I shared some character traits that are quite common among children of survivors. These include a highly protective attitude towards one's parents, the overriding wish being not to add to their pain or disturb whatever peace of mind they might have achieved; a dislike and suspicion of large crowds; and a profound feeling that happiness and security are highly transient, they can be completely wiped out in a moment. But while these feelings ran deep, I wouldn't say that they made my life more difficult than it should have been by some notional standard of normalcy. It may be that my quest to understand traditional religious Judaism intellectually (without also thoroughly living it), to acquire knowledge of part of the world that had been destroyed but in which my parents no longer had any interest, was a form of the "return of the repressed" discussed by Freud. I prefer to think of it as a form of Platonic *eros,* a striving for transcendence, or perhaps Spinoza's intellectual love of God, which has its own peculiar hold on those who have dipped into it. This doesn't mean that I was completely uninterested in definitions of Jewish identity in social, practical, and broadly cultural terms, or in the State of Israel. As a participant in the founding of a Jewish Studies program on the Great Plains of the United States, and director of that program for about twenty years, I did all that I could to foster knowledge of Israeli as well as Jewish history and culture. But these topics have for me always been secondary to the philosophical ones.

Nor have I been very concerned with the postwar histories of Austria and Hungary and their respective policies regarding research on the Holocaust and on public commemorations of the Holocaust, though of course I understand the importance, for later generations especially, of knowing and understanding what happened.[7] But I prefer to focus on the fact that, like many other survivors, rather than emphasizing homelessness and exile, my parents lived and expressed a strong choice for life, in the Biblical (moral) as well as the existential sense. That enabled me to pursue the intellectual interests arising from my own religiously-inclined temperament. I would like my daughter and granddaughter, and perhaps other readers, to be able to keep the example of their resilience in mind. As one of the preeminent sages of antiquity, Rabbi Akiva, saddened by his early lack of education and parental attention, put it: "Happy is the person whose ancestors have gained merit for him. Happy is the person who has a 'peg' on which to hang."

---

[7] An excellent overview of the situation in Hungary is to be found in: Randolph L. Braham and András Kovács (eds.), *The Holocaust in Hungary-Seventy Years Later* (Budapest-New York: Central European University Jewish Studies Program and Central European University Press, 2016). As is well known, similar issues have arisen in other parts of postwar Eastern Europe.

One final point concerning spelling: I have chosen to spell the word "antisemitism' without capitalization or hyphenation, despite the fact that important dictionaries use the long-standing 'anti-Semitism.' My intention is to avoid an obsolete and/or fictitious racial category. It is also the spelling utilized by one of the foremost journals in the academic field of antisemitism studies. The photograph on the front cover shows the distinctive roof of the Hotel Dacia.

I Narrative

Father

Czernowitz and Vienna: Father's Early Years

My father, David Robert Axelrad, was born in Czernowitz in the Bukovina, an area in what is now western Ukraine. At that time, 1910, the town and region were part of the Austro-Hungarian Empire, and like many such towns and regions was multi-ethnic: Germans, Jews, Poles, Ukrainians and others were represented. The imperial government in Vienna made efforts at "Germanization" through educational and cultural policies, and Viennese cultural life was indeed the lodestar for many of the inhabitants of Czernowitz, at least until the Romanian takeover in 1918. As the Austro-Romanian writer Gregor von Rezzori put it, in 1914: "A dozen of the most various nationalities lived there, and a half dozen religions grimly attacking one another; [they coexisted] in a cynical harmony of mutual antipathy and reciprocal deal-making."[8] In 1910, Jews made up about 40 percent of the population, with some speaking mainly German, others mainly Yiddish. As elsewhere in Europe, they were strongly divided between Orthodox and non-Orthodox of various

---

[8] Quoted in: Nataly Shevchenko, Helmut Kusdat, *Das Jüdische Czernowitz Album* (Wien: Album Verlag fur Photographie, 2009), Preface.

kinds. In 1908 the city hosted the World Conference on Yiddish language. It was the birthplace, two years after my father, of Paul Celan, who was to become the preeminent poet of the Shoah. As my father told me, his parents were German speakers originally from Vienna; it is not clear what they were doing in Czernowitz at the time of his birth. Nor is there an explanation for the somewhat unusual spelling of the family name; it was and is more commonly spelled with an "o". In the latter form it may have been of Russian origin, and the final "a" an attempt to Germanize it. It seems that there was an Axelrad, with an "a," family in Czernowitz, which was very well established and sufficiently prosperous to build its own prayer/study house on what is today Ruska Street.[9] A certain Emanuel Axelrad was prominent in the local cement industry. But no connection with this Axelrad family was ever mentioned to me.

My grandfather, Johannes Axelrad, was an industrial chemist. Perhaps he held a position in Czernowitz related to that. His wife Hermine (called Mina) Weissman, was a homemaking perfectionist, reportedly combining apparently both the fabled Germanic cleanliness and rigor (characteristics that would later become distinctly less admirable at the national level) and a Jewish tendency toward overprotectiveness.

Contemplating pictures of Czernowitz today, one sees what one sees in most cities and towns of Eastern Europe: an only partially successful recovery from two totalitarian pasts, with the equivalent of reconstructive surgery plastered over them. No amount of fresh paint and flowers, and restored synagogues, in the fine squares of Krakow, Vilnius, Vienna or Budapest can conceal the artificiality of this renewal. From the former ghetto of Riga and the damp, chill winds blowing over its museum even in summer, to the central square in Szatmárnémeti, where this story will take us, the blood-soaked crimes and psychological and spiritual terrors seeped into the

---

[9] Ibid. photograph #20.

very buildings and streets and remain there. It is as if an inversion had occurred from Moyshe Kulbak's ode (1926) to Jewish Vilnius: "You are a psalm, spelled in clay and iron/Each stone a prayer ." In Czernowitz the former Great Synagogue, built about 1850, set on fire by the Nazis but not entirely destroyed, lives on in misshapen form as a movie theater (as locals apparently call it, the "Kinagoga").

While my father was still a very young child, before 1916, the family moved, or perhaps returned, to Vienna, as thousands of other Eastern European Jews had also recently done and would continue to do after World War I.[10] This rather large migration fuelled an already-existing antisemitism. Nevertheless it was the world of early twentieth- century Vienna that infused my father's character, and that of his younger sister, Emmy, born there. Later, my mother, like many other Central and Eastern European Jews, was to be enormously attracted to Viennese culture and history, to the point of seeking to suppress her Northern Transylvanian origins. Celan described this phenomenon:

"The landscape from which I come to you…was home to a not inconsiderable portion of those Hasidic tales that Martin Buber has retold for us in German. …[T]his former region of the Hapsburg Empire [has] now fallen into historylessness…What was reachable, if distant enough, what had to be reached, was named Vienna. You know how it went then, for years, with this reachability."[11]

A great deal has been written about "fin de siècle Vienna," the Vienna of the 1910s and 1920s. Coming long after Mozart,

---

[10] Cf. Steven Beller, *Vienna and the Jews 1867-1938: A Cultural History* (Cambridge: Cambridge University Press, 1989), 167; Peter Payer, "Judisches Leben in der Brigittenau: Ein Rundgang zu den stummen Zeugen der Vergangenheit," in: Tristan Lehmann (ed.), *Brigittenau: gestern-heute-morgen* (Wien, 1999).

[11] Paul Celan, "Speech on the Occasion of Receiving the Literature Prize of the Free Hanseatic City of Bremen," in: John Felstiner (transl.), *Selected Poems and Prose of Paul Celan* (New York: W.W. Norton & Co., 2001), 395.

Beethoven, Schubert and Haydn in the eighteenth and nineteenth centuries, great composers and musicians lived and performed there in the early twentieth century: Arnold Schoenberg, Gustav Mahler, Alban Berg, and Anton Bruckner, to name only a few. Painters, such as Gustav Klimt and Egon Schiele; writers including Joseph Roth, Stefan Zweig, Arthur Schnitzler, and Karl Kraus; the psychologist Sigmund Freud; the philosopher Ludwig Wittgenstein, all were part of the culture described by a later scholar as "Wittgenstein's Vienna." While the cultural accomplishments were real, the social conditions underlying them were far from unproblematic. Indeed, one historian has argued that: "The German culture and values which the Jews in the Austrian Empire worshipped were something other than reality. They had assimilated into a great and glorious culture but the society for that culture did not exist."[12] Social reality during both the 1920s and 1930s was based on considerable economic hardship in the wake of war and the Great Depression. Housing, infrastructure and employment were utterly inadequate. In addition, political division roiled to the point of actual civil war; Jewish and other ethnic assimilation were at best partial; and there was a pervasive antisemitism whose character easily matched that of the German National Socialists.

Jews had been expelled from Vienna in 1669, and were only permitted to return on a limited basis until the liberal revolutions of 1848. After 1848, they received further civic recognition and rights, but seem never to have reached a high level of organized communal identity such as existed in Prague and Budapest. In 1897, a Jewish parliamentary representative for the city district of Leopoldstadt (the II. District), from the Liberal party, stated despairingly:

"When you consider the way in which the poor Jews strive to gain your {the Austrian society represented by the other deputies] favor in the ranks of the [ethnic] Germans, how they try to accumulate

---

[12] Beller, *Vienna and the Jews*, 164.

the treasures of German culture, how they work in the sciences, some perhaps dying young as a result- and all the thanks they get is that they are not even accepted as human beings."[13]

According to my father's account, the family resided in this Second District, not too far from the *Stefansdom* and inner city or city center. The Second District included the Jewish quarter, Leopoldstadt, as well as the well-known *Judenplatz*. The family probably moved there sometime after the end of World War I, since (judging by an address given on a school certificate) in 1917 they appear to have lived in what is now called Brigittenau, the XX. District. This was an area which was adjacent to the Second District but had been split off from it in the year 1900. My father subsequently entered a *Bundesrealschule* in the XX. District in the academic year 1920-21, at the age of ten. *Realschulen* were a type of secondary school with a strong scientific and practical orientation. He graduated from there in June 1927 with an overall standing of "Very Good." Toward this graduation he completed a special project in physics entitled "The physical and technical significance of steam." Like the education described by Stefan Zweig in *Die Welt von Gestern* (1941), my father's education seems to have been almost completely "European," and only minimally Jewish. Nonetheless a tutor came to the house to prepare my father for his *bar mitzvah*; whether or when this actually took place is unknown.

The Rise of Austro-Fascism

Probably the following year, in 1928, at the age of eighteen, my father entered the Technical University of Vienna, the *Technische Hochschule in Wien*, on the *Karlsplatz*. Although he was an excellent pianist and would have liked to pursue a career in music, his mother wouldn't hear of it, probably a wise decision under the

---

[13] Ibid., 163.

circumstances. In any case, an identity card from the university affirms that he passed the state examination in mechanical engineering (*Maschinenbau*) on 6 July 1936, and now officially held the rank of engineer.

My father described this state examination to me, and indeed the short preceding paragraph conceals an enormous amount about the political and social changes in Vienna and Austria about that time, i.e. the the late 1920s through the late 1930s. It took eight years for my father to obtain this degree, perhaps because it was a combined degree of some kind, but perhaps because of severe economic hardship in Austria and because of antisemitic persecution. Or a combination of these factors. His own father was having a great deal of difficulty remaining in work, again partly because of depressed economic circumstances and in part because of anti-Jewish discrimination. The Depression affected Austria more severely than many other countries:

"By 1934, 44.5% of all industrial workers had been laid off, 34.8% in non-agricultural vocations. Regionally, the slump had its greatest impact in Vienna, in older industrial cities like Wiener Neustadt and Steyr, and in a whole string of textile mining and steel communities in the deep valleys of Styria...In some factory towns of Carinthia and Salzburg the entire population was unemployed."[14]

My father could barely afford to attend the university, and had to sell lecture notes and give English lessons in order to help support himself and his family. (Presumably he had learned English in the *Realschule*.) Not- infrequent physical assaults on Jewish students forced them to stay away; my father would sometimes receive warnings about impending attacks from sympathetic non-Jewish friends. Course work was graded in unfair ways, forcing my father and no

---

[14] Evan Bukey, *Hitler's Austria: popular sentiment in the Nazi era, 1938-1945* (Charlotte: University of North Carolina Press, 2002), 37.

doubt others to repeat assignments or even entire courses.[15] At the final oral examination, the topic of which was naturally something entirely scientific, one of the board of examiners posed the question: "How is it that you have a Jewish-sounding name?" To which my father replied: *"Auf diese Frage habe ich mich leider nicht vorbereitet."* (Regrettably, I did not prepare for this question.)

This was by now the Vienna of the rising National Socialist movement; the cosmopolitan, relatively liberal and tolerant capital of the Hapsburg Empire, to the extent that it had ever really existed, had disappeared. The worldwide economic depression and banking crisis reached their height in Austria in the spring of 1931, while the political state of affairs was extremely fractured, indeed chaotic. There were multiple parties, including the conservative Christian Socials, the Social Democrats, and the National Socialists, all operating in an extremely uncompromising manner, and having associated paramilitary wings. In March 1933, the government led by the Chancellor Engelbert Dollfuss (1892-1934) managed, through a parliamentary manoeuvre, to dissolve the parliament altogether and to rule without it on the basis of a war-production act from 1917. This was a move not too dissimilar to what had taken place in Germany beginning in 1932, when Chancellor Brüning requested and received, from the Reich President Hindenburg, a dissolution of the Reichstag. The aim was to short- circuit protracted and intractable inter-party negotiations and compromises.

Meanwhile, during the remainder of the spring and during the summer of 1933, assisted financially by their German counterparts, the Austrian National Socialists were able to continue stepping up violent, subversive and racist activities. They carried out ever more terror attacks, bombing Jewish shops, railroad stations, public telephone booths, and power stations. The German National Socialists

---

[15] Simon Wiesenthal (later famous for his work in tracking Nazi criminals) reported similar difficulties, at roughly the same time, in obtaining his certification in architecture at the University of Lvov.

violated Austrian airspace by flying over and dropping leaflets encouraging civil disobedience, non-payment of taxes and a run on banks.[16]

In September of the same year, having banned both the Communist and the National Socialist parties, Dollfuss declared that Austria would now be an authoritarian "*Ständestaat.*" Roughly translated, this means a corporatist state on the fascist model. Indeed Dollfuss pursued a friendship, if not an alliance, with the fascist dictator of Italy, Benito Mussolini. This was probably, in part, to differentiate his regime from that of Hitler and to fend off the Austrian National Socialists. Nonetheless, installations were constructed to house internal political opponents. A small civil war between Leftists and Rightists broke out in February 1934, leaving hundreds of civilians dead. As in neighboring Germany, and as would happen in Hungary and elsewhere in Central and Eastern Europe, civic strife between Left-leaning and socialist political movements, on the one hand, and far-Right National Socialist ones on the other, not only increasingly empoisoned the general atmosphere and made violence pervasive, but squeezed and reduced the influence of relatively more moderate conservative parties. After the fighting ended in February, the German National Socialists moved quickly to defend the Austrian fighters in court, to provide assistance to those who had been detained, and to conceal the escape of the Upper Austrian militia commander (Richard Bernaschek) to Germany.[17] At this point Mussolini decided to support his Austrian colleagues by sending troops to block the Brenner Pass and potential German troop movements. Such movements did not materialize just at this moment, but would do so four years later. Dollfuss was assassinated

---

[16] Thomas Weyr, *The Setting of the Pearl: Vienna Under Hitler* (Oxford: Oxford University Press, 2005),54; Sonia Wachstein, *Too Deep Were Our Roots: A Viennese Jewish Memoir of the Years Between the Two World Wars* (Harbor Electronic Publishing, 2001).

[17] Bukey, *Hitler's Austria*, 41.

on 25 July 1934, in the course of a failed coup by the Nazis. He was replaced as Chancellor by Karl Schuschnigg.

By 1935, industrial output in Austria had fallen to levels below those of the 1920s, unemployment was higher than it had been in 1933, and exports had fallen by 50 percent of recent years. In the summer of 1936 (just when my father received his engineering degree), an agreement was drawn up between Austria and Germany. By the terms of the agreement Germany recognized Austria's formal independence, but German influence would be exercised indirectly through the appointment to the government of two members of the "national opposition," i.e. the National Socialists. Further, Austria's foreign policy would be closely aligned with that of Germany; and National Socialists currently imprisoned would be released immediately. While this arrangement meant that the German government was apparently providing assurance that it would not interfere in Austrian politics, there was no such assurance regarding the German National Socialists (NSDAP). Indeed the NSDAP sent financial aid to the Austrian Nazis, sent personnel, and helped reorganize the Austrian SS and SA. The Austrian groups were so fanatical that they ended up in violent clashes with the German Hitler Youth.[18]

The Anschluss-- Family Departure

Nor did this "indirect" German influence last long as such. By November 1937 Hitler was laying out plans for a longer -term "relationship" with Austria: he envisioned a customs and currency union, as well as territorial integration of the Sudetenland and Austria into the German Reich. The head of the German Air Force (*Luftwaffe*) and co-leader of economic planning, Hermann Göring, visited Mussolini (Hitler's ally) to explain to him that Germany needed

---

[18] Weyr, *Setting*, 60.

Austria's timber, gold, coal, iron and hydro-electric power.[19] Later, on the eve of the German invasion of Hungary in 1944, it would again be Göring who insisted on the need to exploit (other nations') available natural resources for the war effort. Under pressure from Berlin, through the mediation of Franz von Papen (formerly German Chancellor and now German Ambassador to Austria), Hitler and Schuschnigg met at Hitler's favorite spot, his home in Berchtesgarden, Bavaria, on 12 February 1938. Briefly stated, for various reasons, but heavily pressured by Göring, Hitler threatened invasion of Austria, and Schuschnigg agreed to the appointment of Arthur Seyss-Inquart, a National Socialist sympathizer, as Austrian Minister of the Interior. After this meeting, perhaps feeling that he had gone too far, or because he sought greater legitimacy for his government, Schuschnigg decided to call a plebiscite on the continuing independence of Austria. He set the date for Sunday, 13 March 1938.

It was quite widely expected that, while the National Socialists would win a substantial number of votes, ultimately the Christian Socials would carry the day. In one historian's assessment:

"...while it is unlikely that Austrians would have given Nazi candidates sufficient support to bring them to power {in free parliamentary elections], there can be no doubt that most of the populace looked favorably on a merger with Germany as a way out of their chaotic conditions."[20]

Meanwhile, antisemitic sentiment had continued to increase since World War I. As mentioned earlier, the migration of Jews from Galicia, Romania and other Eastern lands toward Vienna before the war had already led to heightened antisemitic attitudes. During and immediately after the war, severe food, housing and fuel shortages, together with political confusion arising from the collapse of empires and the setting up of communist revolutionary councils (especially in large cities such as Vienna) greatly added to the hostility toward

[19] Ibid.
[20] Bukey, *Hitler's Austria*, 41.

Jews. Jews were widely perceived as being responsible for both the catastrophic military defeat of 1918 and the revolutionary councils of the immediate postwar period. Demands began to be made for anti-Jewish legislation.[21]

Two days before the planned vote on a merger with Germany, on 11 March 1938, Hitler again threatened military action. With Göring directing events by telephone from Berlin, Schuschnigg very reluctantly resigned as Chancellor in favor of Seyss-Inquart, while the plebiscite was called off. On 12 March, a large contingent of SS troops marched into Austria, followed by regular Wehrmacht soldiers. As is well-known, they received a rapturous welcome along the invasion route and especially in Vienna, possibly even to Hitler's own surprise. The German writer and playwright Carl Zuckmayr, who had already fled from Hitler's Germany into Austria (and would later emigrate to the United States) described these events as follows:

"What it was like in reality (or rather, in the lived dreams which we want to call reality), how it actually happened—this is something that only those who went through it can possibly know…"[22]

"That night hell broke loose. The underworld opened its gates and vomited forth the lowest, filthiest, most horrible demons it contained. The city was transformed into a nightmare painting by Hieronymous Bosch: phantoms and devils seemed to have crawled out from sewers and swamps. The air was filled with an incessant screeching, horrible, piercing, hysterical cries from the throats of men and women who continued screaming day and night. People's faces vanished, and were replaced by contorted masks, some of fear, some of cunning, some of wild, hate-filled triumph."[23]

"What was unleashed upon Vienna had nothing to do with [Hitler's] seizure of power in Germany, which proceeded under the guise of legality and was met by parts of the population with

---

[21] Ibid., 43.
[22] Zuckmayr quoted in Bukey, *Hitler's Austria*, 27.
[23] Ibid., 28.

alienation, skepticism, or an unsuspecting nationalistic idealism. What was unleashed in Vienna was a torrent of envy, jealousy, bitterness, blind, malignant craving for revenge."[24]

And, I would have added, an exact mirror of Hitler's own personality.

The journalist William Shirer, best known for his books *The Rise and Fall of the Third Reich* and *Berlin Diary*, saw "young toughs heaving paving blocks into the windows of Jewish shops" on or near the elegant, central Kärntnerstrasse. "The Brownshirts at Nuremberg had never bellowed Nazi slogans with such mania."[25] Further down Kärntnerstrasse, near the iconic *Stefansdom*, another journalist described

"a stream of humanity...hooting furiously, trying to make themselves heard above the din, men and women leaping, shouting and dancing in the light of the smoking torches which soon began to make their appearance, the air filled with...screams of 'Down with the Jews! Heil Hitler! *Sieg heil!* Perish the Jews!...Hang Schuschnigg! Heil Seyss-Inquart! Down with the Catholics! *Ein Volk, ein Reich, ein Fuhrer!*"[26]

Hitler, now a triumphant returnee to a city which had seen his abject failures in the 1920s, gave a rousing speech at the *Heldenplatz* near the Imperial Palace (*Hofburg*). In the speech he emphasized the ethnic unity of German-speaking peoples and Austria's role as the *Ostmark,* the easternmost reaches of German empires. Although he could have spent the night in an apartment of the *Hofburg*, he made a point of staying at the Hotel Imperial, where he had once been hired to sweep the snowy sidewalk, as dignitaries came and went.

From this moment on, non-Jews were required to display their Aryan status with a swastika-button; Jews were removed from the civil service, from jobs and occupations in the private and professional

---

[24] Ibid.
[25] Ibid., 45.
[26] Ibid.,46.

sectors, and were deprived of their various forms of property by both lawful (under the new regime) and unlawful means. Jews, especially in those concentrated in Leopoldstadt (the II. District), suffered frequent assaults and home-invasions by hoodlums and thugs; they were forced to perform degrading acts such as scrubbing sidewalks and public toilets; and they were forbidden to sit down on benches in the many beautiful public parks of the city.

Under the circumstances, while some Viennese Jews were either unable or unwilling to leave Austria, many made rapid efforts toward departure: to England or Western Europe, to Palestine, or to other points east. My father's family— his father, mother, sister and now brother-in-law Feri Mandel (an orthopedic surgeon) – decided first to go to Bratislava (Slovakia)) where they had holidayed in the past. It soon became clear to them, however, that here too they were considered undesirables (*unerwünschte Personen*), and so they decided to move on to Turkey. They were able to board a train in that direction. But at some point along the journey, a fellow-passenger persuaded them to make a stop in Szatmár, Northern Transylvania (at that point part of Romania). He (the fellow-passenger) had contacts in the Jewish community there and could help them find temporary shelter. Perhaps out of fatigue, or because they accepted the view, widespread in the Hungarian-speaking Jewish community, that the Hungarian government would be able to lend them some protection and that Hitler's reach would somehow not extend to them, they agreed. They descended from the train in Szatmárnémeti. This would have been sometime in the summer or fall of 1938.

First Years in Szatmárnémeti

Initially, my father again took up English tutoring as a means of subsistence. But gradually he found work at *Reiter Viktor & Söhne Zuckerfabrik*, a sugar factory belonging to a relative of my maternal grandmother, Rozsa Reiter, and also at *ICA Chemische Werke (Industria Chemicale Ardeleana)*. It is not clear in which order he was employed at these two places. Much later, at the time of applying for reparations, it became a question for the German lawyers handling the case as to whether he had been paid in Hungarian currency, *pengös,* or in Romanian *lei,* as if there was a big difference.

Romania had ruled this area of Northern Transylvania since the conclusion of the Versailles Treaty negotiations after World War I. The Treaty of Trianon (1920) carved up Hungary, such that Transylvania (both North and South) and the southern Bánság/Banat region were awarded to Romania; the western Burgenland went to Austria; and Croatia-Slavonia went to Yugoslavia. For various, not altogether clear reasons, Hitler intervened in ongoing disputes between Hungary and Romania regarding these territorial arrangements and other matters between 1938 and 1940. In August-September 1940, on the basis of the Second Vienna Award "mediated" by Germany and Italy, Northern Transylvania, including the cities of Szatmárnémeti and Kolozsvár (in Romanian Cluj, considered the capital of the region), was returned to Hungary; Romania unhappily received Southern Transylvania. Hitler seems to have wanted to leverage the permanent strife between the two countries to obtain concrete support for his war plans; by playing them off against one another in the intense and longstanding struggle for Transylvania and other areas, he could obtain men and materiel from the two countries, as well as transit rights for German troops. Indeed, Romania relatively quickly committed 700,000 troops to the conquest of the Soviet Union. Hungary, however, proved less compliant.[27] Minutes from a conversation between Hitler and Franz Halder, Chief of Staff of the German Army High Command, in February 1941, suggest that

---

[27] Cf. Mario D. Fenyö, *Hitler, Horthy, and Hungary: German-Hungarian Relations,1941-1944* (New Haven: Yale University Press, 1972), Ch.1; Holly Case, *Between States: The Transylvanian Question and the European Idea During World War II* (Stanford: Stanford University Press, 2009), 70-75.

at first Hitler did not seem overly concerned about Hungary's pre-
varication. Apparently at that stage he regarded Romania as much
more important for the war in the East, and was simply rather irked
by Hungary's "close connection to countries hostile to Germany."[28]
Nonetheless from the beginning he wanted transit rights through
Hungary both on the ground and in the air, and gradually increased
the pressure. In a letter to Admiral Horthy, the Hungarian head
of state, in December 1941, Hitler stated that "my candid wish...
is that Hungarian units may participate in the decisive fight once
again in the coming year."[29] In other words, transit rights were no
longer enough, troops and equipment were expected. This letter was
followed up by a visit to Horthy from the German Foreign Minister,
Joachim von Ribbentrop, in January 1942. During the visit, the
need for active Hungarian military participation in the war in the
Soviet Union was emphatically conveyed, and the German military
attaché in Budapest was tasked with keeping the Hungarian government informed, on a daily basis, about progress in the southern
sector of the Eastern front. During a similar visit of "encouragement"
to Romania by Field Marshal Wilhelm Keitel, in the same month,
the Romanians complained bitterly about Hungarian evasion of
military commitments. The Hungarians decided they had better
undertake some definite action in this regard, and in the spring of
1942 Hungarian military preparations began in earnest.

The reasons for Hungary's fateful decision at this point to ramp
up its war effort in support of Germany and against the Soviet Union
were complex. It is hard to know how to weight the different factors. One extremely strong motivation was to stay on Hitler's good
side, so to speak, in order to obtain further revision of the Trianon
Treaty, that is to say, further return of lands which had been ceded to
other countries. Although the Hungarians had recovered Northern
Transylvania, they still hoped to win back the southern portion,

[28] Fenyö, *Hitler, Horthy*,14.
[29] Quoted in Ibid., 35.

along with territories on other borders. As Prime Minister Miklós Kallay later wrote in his memoirs: "Practically the sole reason why we entered the war and sent an army against the Russians was that the Rumanians were already taking part with full force against the Russians, whereas we were not, and thus we risked losing German favor and Transylvania."[30] But there were other considerations too, perhaps even more important. There was fear of a Soviet victory, and with it not only re-occupation of parts of Eastern Europe by the Russians, who had shown themselves to be extremely brutal occupiers, but the longer-term establishment of communism. Further, Hungary and Germany had become increasingly inter-dependent economically throughout the 1930s and especially after 1938. The vast majority of Hungary's agricultural and mineral exports went to Germany; by 1942, the trade surplus was running very much in Hungary's favor. In return, Hungary received armaments, machines, trucks and industrial goods.[31] Finally, not to be overlooked, was no doubt a certain sympathy for the fascist worldview represented by Hitler, despite the fact that Admiral Horthy and other members of the Hungarian ruling elite came from a conservative aristocratic class that was in many ways disapproving of the Hitlerian regime. In any case, as the war went on, not only Hungarian troops but Hungarian oil and bauxite came to be seen, especially by Göring, as vital to the German war effort, and Hitler became more and more explicit in his demands.

In the course of their altered lives in Szatmár, either through some in the Jewish upper bourgeoisie who wanted to learn English, or through Jewish civic organizations, or through some other means, my father and his family came into contact with that of my mother.

---

[30] Quoted in ibid., 41.

[31] Christian Gerlach und Götz Aly, *Das letzte Kapitel: Der Mord an den ungarischen Juden 1944-1945* (Frankfurt am Main: Fischer Taschenbuch Verlag, 2004), 28.

But at this point they were merely quite casual acquaintances, moving in a broadly similar social circle.

As more than one scholar has noted, "it is one of the ironies of history that after the 1940 division of Transylvania, the Jews fared worse in Northern Transylvania, in the part allotted to Hungary, than in the part left to Romania, which was more identified with antisemitic excesses." [32] Throughout the 1930s, both countries pursued increasingly anti-Jewish policies, but Hungarian Jews, including those in Northern Transylvania, clung to the belief that their long history of acculturation, Magyarization, military service, and so on, would protect them to some extent economically and legally. They continued to believe or hope that the Parliament, the Regent and other components of the ruling class remained on the whole moderate; that anti-Jewish laws and actions would not attain the German level; and that their way of life could continue tolerably. The truth was that the seeming moderates, including the Regent Horthy, "were willing to sacrifice Hungarian Jewry to the exigencies of the German alliance and the need to buy off the radical Right by passing anti-Jewish laws."[33] Moreover, conservative Hungarian leaders tended to insist on a distinction between Hungarian Jews and "Galicians," or Jews from Poland and further East, usually Orthodox; this may have lulled long-established Hungarian Jews into what turned out to be a false sense of security. The city of Szatmárnémeti itself, like Czernowitz and many other places, was sharply divided between Orthodoxy and the more liberal Neolog movement. Be that as it may, by making this distinction the so-called moderate conservatives thought they could both show that they were not antisemitic and at the same time pursue anti-Jewish

---

[32] Randolph L. Braham (ed.), *Genocide and Retribution: The Holocaust in Hungarian-Ruled Northern Transylvania* (Boston: Kluwer, 1983), 8; Ezra Mendelsohn, *The Jews of East Central Europe Between the World Wars* (Bloomington: Indiana University Press, 1982), 98.

[33] Mendelsohn, *East Central Europe*, 127.

policies. It was not unusual to hear repeated the opinion of Count István Bethlen, Prime Minister of Hungary from 1921 to 1931: "The essence of the Jewish problem is that there are too many of them and their influence is too great."[34] As had occurred in Austria, during the period 1938-1940 in Hungary, all moderate journalistic and civil society voices were suppressed; Jews were dismissed from the civil service and the professions; Jewish students were excluded from universities and professional schools and discriminated against in the secondary schools; and various forms of property owned by Jews were increasingly threatened or confiscated.

Hungary, the Eastern Front, and the Labor Service System

Although Hungary had officially declared war on the Soviet Union on 27 June 1941, that is, five days after the start of Operation Barbarossa by the Germans, it had only sent a small number of troops initially and had managed, by various subterfuges, to bring those home quite quickly. But by the spring of 1942, as we saw above, the German government started to exert fresh pressure on the Hungarian government to contribute to the war effort at a much higher level, especially on the Eastern front. The Hungarians decided to "ramp up" the labor service company mechanism which had been in existence since the early 1920s.[35] At that time, the

---

[34] Bethlen quoted in Mendelsohn, *Jews of East Central Europe*,121.

[35] The following account of the labor service system is based on one of only a few studies on this topic: Randolph L. Braham, *The Hungarian Labor Service System 1939-1945* (East European Quarterly, distributed by Columbia University Press, 1977). See also László Csösa, "The Origins of the Military Labor Service System in Hungary," in: Braham and Kovacs (eds.), *The Holocaust in Hungary*, 75-104. Robert Rozett has recently provided an updated account, including some survivor testimony in *Conscripted Slaves: Hungarian Jewish Forced Laborers on the Eastern Front during the Second World War* (Jerusalem: Yad Vashem, 2013).

Hungarian Ministry of War had placed "politically unreliable men" (not necessarily Jews) of military age into special units – "labor detachments"—that would perform various military support functions. This was a practice which was implemented by other nations as well.[36] The men in these detachments would wear civilian clothing but have armbands showing their status, and they would not be permitted to carry weapons. The first such detachment had been organized by Admiral Miklós Horthy in December 1919, during the counterrevolution against the Communist regime of Béla Kun. This was the very same Horthy of Nagybánya who served as Regent from 1920 to 1944 (technically representing the monarch Charles IV Apostolic King of Hungary, who was not able to retain the throne after World War I) and who was supposedly a moderate conservative, with no abnormal antipathy to assimilated Jews. Given how the labor service system actually functioned during World War II, however, it is difficult to see how this reputation for moderation could have come about.

The labor service system in support of the military was revived in July 1939 through Anti-Jewish Law No. II. The law dealt with many topics relating to national defense, including the granting of emergency powers to the government, in addition to the compulsory labor service system. Under the system, "unreliables" were considered to include Romanians, Slovaks, Serbs and Jews, but Jews came in for added restrictions: no Jews could serve as officers; they could not do any work related to intelligence or administration; they could not serve as couriers or work in warehouses. The aim from the outset seems to have been not only to prevent Jews from coming anywhere near useful or important information, but to subject them to the physically harshest measures possible. And, as we shall see, this aim was fulfilled to the most terrible extent.

The men in the labor service system were organized into eight

---

[36] Csösz, "Origins".

battalions, which were further sub-divided into platoons and companies of 200 to 250 men each. They were "armed" with shovels, pickaxes and the like, and were placed in either domestic labor or field labor companies. The former consisted more of older and weaker men, the latter of the younger and stronger. In 1942 there were about 100,000 men in the labor service system controlled by the Hungarian Army; within that total were about 52,000 Jews in two hundred and sixty companies.[37] Initially the Jewish companies were distributed throughout Hungary, but this changed as the Hungarian Government decided to, or was constrained to, demonstrate more concrete support for the German advances in the Soviet Union. The Second Hungarian Army was called up and deployed to lend (largely) logistical support to the German Sixth Army, which was operating in Ukraine and in southern Russia. Labor battalions, including my father's, were sent along with the Second Hungarian Army.

The tasks of the labor service companies were various but always arduous. During the first six months or so of the war with the Soviet Union, the labor companies were tasked, first, with building and maintaining the roads and bridges that connected Hungary proper with Hungarian-occupied parts of Ukraine.[38] They also cleared forests (for example, on the border between Hungary and Romania) for ease of troop movement and to prevent partisans from hiding; dredged rivers; unloaded freight at railyards; built and maintained airfields; worked in convalescent hospitals; and performed agricultural labor on large landed estates.

Before 1942, and during the spring of that year, Jews assigned to a job location near their homes were permitted to sleep and eat at home; others were generally permitted to write and send letters home. Exemptions could also sometimes be arranged, that is, bought. But after spring 1942, things would change dramatically and tragically for the worse.

---

[37] Braham, *Hungarian Labor Service*, 19.

[38] Ibid., 32.

My father, as he briefly recounted it, was somewhere in Ukraine, doing road work, though his reparations claim statement also mentions the Carpathians; heavy road work was indeed also being done along the Carpathian Mountain passes as well as in Ukraine. While initially in all zones the laborers had fairly adequate (civilian) clothing, in the course of the fall and winter of 1942, clothing and boots wore out as the laborers were driven eastward through long marches, and were subjected to unspeakable cruelties. They did very heavy labor all day in the wintry outdoors, receiving either meager food rations or none at all. Not infrequently they were forced to perform "calisthenics" for the entertainment of Hungarian officers at the end of the day. In the course of the winter (1942-1943) many of the Jewish labor service men died. Jewish laborers who had converted to Christianity at some earlier time were sometimes able to avoid service in Ukraine or elsewhere on the front, and received some aid from Christian churches. Jewish aid organizations also managed to provide some supplies, but they were facing enormous difficulties of their own and it was far too little.[39]

During the organization of the labor service companies attached to the Second Hungarian Army, a visible effort had been made to recruit Jews from the professions, from industry and commerce, adherents of Zionist parties, and community leaders in general. Denunciations of Jews were made by covetous neighbors who anticipated being able to take over their businesses; by supporters of extreme Right parties and associations; and by local professional organizations, who also had their eyes on the practices of their medical, legal and engineering colleagues. Old, infirm and sick Jews were called up as readily as young and fit ones.

The Second Hungarian Army was deployed on 11 April 1942,

---

[39] Some discussion of the attitudes and actions of the Christian churches in Hungary in relation to the labor battalions can be found in: Paul Hanebrink, *In Defense of Christian Hungary: Religion, Nationalism and Antisemitism, 1890-1944* (Ithaca: Cornell University Press, 2006),202.

with 250,000 soldiers and 50,000 Jewish labor servicemen. It was ordered to provide logistical and disciplinary support to the (German) Army Group South (*Heeresgruppe Sud*) under Field Marshall Maximilian von Weichs. The Second Hungarian Army itself, however, was poorly equipped, having wholly inadequate winter clothing, food, heating fuel and building supplies. It had to march one thousand kilometers to the front in Ukraine, arriving there about 27 June 1942. By 10 July it reached the Don River, south of Voronezh.

My father's exact fate on the Eastern front is difficult to ascertain. He himself said almost nothing about the details. However, he did talk of eventually escaping from his labor service unit, hiding out in the "Russian" [possibly he meant to say Ukrainian or Soviet] countryside for several months, and then with two other companions managing to get back, mainly on foot, to Hungary. The ability to hide for extended periods of time would tend to support Robert Rozett's contention that the local Ukrainian population was not always as hostile as it is generally thought to have been. Rozett also raises the possibility that the local Ukrainian peasants may not have at first realized that the escapees they helped – i.e. Hungarian Jewish labor service prisoners they encountered-- were Jewish. But on the whole such benevolent treatment, or the occasional reprieve through a German Wehrmacht soldier, was not common.[40]

It is possible that my father had actually deployed before the Hungarian declaration of war against the Soviet Union (27 June 1941), and had escaped into the Soviet Union, along with many other servicemen, in May-June 1941. This is possible since the Hungarian Ministry of Defense had re-started the labor service system first in connection with the conflict with Romania, and border-clearing work had begun not long thereafter (fall 1940). However, I think it more likely, given the work record as reported in his reparations claim-- where 1942 is the year he gave as the beginning of his

---

[40] Rozett, *Conscripted Slaves*, 171-173.

enslavement-- and given the process of Hungarian army recruitment in spring 1942, that he entered the labor service at that point and worked on the German-Hungarian invasion path into Soviet territory, probably somewhere along a border with Ukraine. Conditions experienced by the labor servicemen were already extremely harsh, and this would certainly have been a motive to escape, if one were needed. Therefore I surmise that he was part of the spring 1942 deployment with the Second Hungarian Army, and that the escape he referred to took place during the German-Hungarian retreat from Voronezh (12 January 1943), not long before the ultimate, even more catastrophic defeat at Stalingrad (February 1943).

The hard labor done by the Jewish Hungarian labor servicemen and the atrocities suffered by them both before and after Voronezh are difficult to summarize. Here is another description from the principal authority on the subject, Randolph Braham:

"In the Ukraine, the labor service companies had been employed on a variety of projects specified by the Hungarian and German military authorities. They included the clearing and maintenance of roads and railroads, including snow removal; the loading and unloading of munitions, provisions and other materials; and war-related technical works [my father mentioned that his engineering degree was deemed useful here], including the building of trenches, tank traps, bunkers and gun emplacements, and the removal of mines from the fields. ...The various types of fortification work were extraordinarily demanding in winter, when the soil was frozen and the shovels and pickaxes wielded by the emaciated labor servicemen could hardly penetrate it. The clearing of minefields, which sometimes meant marching over them, exacted an especially large number of casualties. Often the labor service companies were made to assist horse-drawn supply trains, especially along the passes and the muddy roads, and on many occasions they were actually forced to replace the horses that collapsed or died of exhaustion.

Some especially sadistic commanders made them pull the heavily laden wagons 'to save the energy of the animals.'"[41]

In addition to the extreme physical hardship of the war effort suffered by the labor service men, they also had to endure vicious antisemitism on the part of both Hungarian company commanders and German SS and military police. They were on the receiving end of incessant abuse, torture and humiliation. For example, the servicemen, freezing in their fragmentary clothing, starving, and infested with lice, would often be kicked out of whatever shelters they had during the night and be forced to give them up to Hungarian or German soldiers. In spite of all this, senior commanders in the Second Hungarian Army were forced to recognize that in the course of the retreat from Voronezh, beginning with the successful Soviet offensive on 12 January 1943,

"...these Jews [the labor servicemen] are much more disciplined than our *Honveds* [non-Jewish Hungarian soldiers]. ...The Jews brought out the wounded and the dead *Honveds* in the midst of the greatest fire."[42]

The Hungarian Army took great losses here: about 130,000-140,000 men died.

Apart from losses sustained in the recovery actions they undertook, the Jewish labor companies naturally lost huge numbers to hunger, extreme cold and disease, especially typhoid fever.

"In the absence of hospitals or medication, many died by the wayside. In some cases, labor servicemen ill with typhoid were ordered to run for fifteen minutes together with their healthy comrades, then 'bathe' in the ice-cold river [possibly the Don or one of its tributaries] and stand naked in the wind for inspection by the sadistic guards."[43]

A "final solution" to the typhoid problem was found at Dorosic,

---

[41] Ibid., 32.

[42] Ibid., 38.

[43] Ibid., 39.

west of Kiev in Ukraine. This was a small staging or holding area
for retreating Jewish Hungarian labor servicemen. A makeshift hospital had been set up there in an effort at some sort of quarantine,
but most of the ill servicemen lay in open barns nearby. Getting
fed up with a medical process that seemed to them overly long,
the Hungarian guards decided, on 19 April 1943 (the last day of
Passover and the day on which final deportations from the Warsaw
Ghetto commenced), to set the barns on fire. Since the whole area
was fenced off with barbed wire, the men who tried to run out of
the barns and were in many case alight with fire could not escape.
About 600 were burned to death or machine-gunned.

Altogether only about 6,000-7,000 of the original 50,000 Jewish
labor servicemen survived both the invasion of and retreat from
the Soviet Union and returned to Hungary. "In the chaos that followed the Voronezh debacle, many labor service companies simply
disintegrated. Thousands were killed at the battle of the Don; tens
of thousands were captured by the victorious Soviet forces; tens of
thousands retreated in disorganized, leaderless fashion."[44] Many
labor service company commanders left their posts. My father, as
has been mentioned, escaped at some point, and, as he told me,
managed to get back to Budapest on his own. I don't know where he
stayed or hid during that time; he did mention hiding out in barns
on Russian and Ukrainian farms. But this was by no means the end
of his terrible suffering.

In the meantime, according to my father (and as someone must
have told him subsequently, after the war was over), my paternal
grandparents had decided to make a return trip to Vienna, while
they could still obtain permission from the Hungarian government to travel. They hoped to retrieve some belongings from their
apartment. It appears that while there they died in the course of
a bombardment of the city. This probably happened in the fall of

---

[44] Ibid., 37.

1942, as consistent bombing of Vienna – for a total of fifty-two bombardments—began on 4 September of that year. The targets were mainly oil refineries: the Loban, Moosbier, Florisdorf and other refineries were hit. Florisdorf is not too far from Brigittenau. I don't know whether or not Emmy (my father's sister) and her husband Feri accompanied the parents to Vienna. If they did, they were likely caught up in the same bombardment. If not, Emmy was most likely deported along with the other Jews living in Szatmár in 1944, while Feri would have been placed in a labor service battalion around 1942. But nothing is known of their fates.

On 19 March 1944 Germany invaded Hungary. As with most such decisions, the reasons for it were numerous and quite complex. Hitler had not trusted Horthy and the Hungarian government since at least 1938, when he deemed Horthy's response to the Sudetenland crisis (during which Germany sought to take control of several German-speaking areas of Czechoslovakia) to be insufficiently supportive. Hitler's exact word for the Hungarian response was "listless".[45] The fact that the Jewish population of Hungary was still largely intact was also deemed intolerable. Hitler wanted to see an intensification of anti-Jewish policy in Hungary, indeed the complete "de-Jewification" of the country.[46] Further, the German Foreign Ministry had caught wind of Hungarian approaches to the Allies. Germany was determined to prevent Hungary from changing sides in the war: above all, Hitler wanted to retain access to, if not control over, Hungary's vital oil, bauxite and timber industries, as well its farmlands. At a series of meetings in Budapest and elsewhere in Hungary, including the town of Szatmárnémeti, in early and

---

[45] Andreas Hillgruber (Hrsg.), *Staatsmänner und Diplomaten bei Hitler: Vertrauliche Aufzeichnungen über Unterredungen mit Vertretern des Auslandes 1942-1944* (Frankfurt am Main: Bernard & Graefe Verlag für Wehrwesen, 1970), 260.

[46] Cf. Richard J. Evans, *The Third Reich at War 1939-1945* (New York: Penguin Books, 2008), 395.

mid-April 1944, the placing of the entire Hungarian Jewish population into ghettos, and subsequent deportation to Auschwitz and other death camps, was planned and organized. I shall return to this process presently. My father, subsisting somehow and somewhere in Budapest after his escape from Ukraine and Russia, was now one of the approximately 220,000 Jews in Budapest who would either undergo the ghettoization and deportation process, or be sent out on a forced march, an indescribable ordeal.

Death Marches: Budapest- Nagy-Czenk
(Gross-Zinkendorf)-Mauthausen[47]

On 15 June 1944 came the order to concentrate the Jews of Budapest into a few districts, with some "international" Jews, i.e. holders of foreign passports or other papers, being placed in designated buildings in a certain area, and all others in a large ghetto near the grand Dohányi Street Synagogue. The international ghetto held about 20-30,000 Jews, the larger ghetto about 70,000.

During these spring and early summer months, however, the political constellation of forces within the Hungarian government was also changing. By mid-October, with Soviet forces having entered eastern Hungary, Hitler's chief representative (Reich Plenipotentiary), SS Brigadeführer Edmund Veesenmeyer forced Regent Horthy to disband the existing government and appoint a Prime Minister and cabinet from the extreme Right Arrow Cross Party. He accomplished

---

[47] An interesting problem arises with the stating of camp names. On the one hand, giving the local-language name (in this case the Hungarian name) indicates the territorial location and preserves a sense of nationality – both positive and negative aspects. On the other hand, giving the German names underscores that the Germans were ultimately the instigators of the entire camp system, obviously an important consideration. I have decided to provide Hungarian names first, with German names following, mainly to facilitate understanding of geography.

this in part by (no doubt) approving the kidnapping of Horthy's younger son (also named Miklós) by German commandos. Miklós Horthy II was immediately taken to Mauthausen and placed in a cell above the gas chamber. On 15 October Ferenc Szálasi, leader of the Arrow Cross Party, was appointed the new Prime Minister and leader of the nation.

At the same time it was decided, at a meeting at the Belvedere Hotel in Budapest between representatives of the Hungarian Ministries of the Interior and Defense (now under Arrow Cross control), and the local head of the Gestapo, SS Brigadeführer Hans Geschke, that approximately 35,000 Budapest Jews, plus 50,000 others who had been intended for Auschwitz, would be used for the ongoing fortification work against the Soviets in the Trans-Danubia region (western Hungary and eastern Lower Austria) instead.[48] The remaining Jews of Budapest, about 160,000, stayed in Budapest over the winter. Many of them died of cold and malnutrition, or from bombardment of the city by the Soviets.

Most of the Jews, including my father, who had been selected for fortification work were marched westward, through the towns of Köszég, Moson and Sopron, near the Hungarian border with Austria; in the fall of 1944, they would be moved on toward the district of Linz, Austria. According to his reparations claim statement, my father participated in one of several forced marches of Jews, mainly but not exclusively men, from Budapest toward the eastern part of Lower Austria. As just mentioned, these marches took place mainly in the summer and fall of 1944, but his had already occurred in January of that year. In January 1944, having probably followed the Györ-Moson-Sopron route that would become quite entrenched, he arrived with his group at the Nagy-Czenk (*Gross Zinkendorf*) labor camp. The camps in the Sopron district - around Lake Fertö (*Neusiedler See*) --were intended to provide labor for

---

[48] Braham, *Labor Service,*74.

defensive fortifications for Vienna and other parts of Austria against the Soviets.

Another, smaller contingent was marched, in the summer of 1944, to the Serbian town and coppermines at Bor. On the return march from Serbia to Hungary, in the fall, the great Hungarian poet Miklós Radnóti composed a number of poems about this particular route. There is, for example, the poem "Postcards III," written at Mohács, a place of great symbolic importance to Hungarians, on 24 October 1944. I quote a small part of it here because it must convey similar tortures endured by the Jews, including my father, marching through Trans-Danubia:

Blood red, the spittle drools from the oxen's mouths,
The men stooping to urinate pass blood,
The squad stands bunched in groups whose reek disgusts,
And loathsome death blows overhead in gusts.[49]

Like many others collapsing from exhaustion, Radnóti received a bullet to the neck and was buried in a mass grave near the road. He was thirty -five. The poems were discovered on his body when mass graves were discovered after the war's end.

The Jews trudging through Trans-Danubia marched in harsh winter conditions (again, my father's contingent in January 1944, the others in fall and winter 1944-1945). They had to work on heavy for-tifications, ditches, tank traps and so on, while receiving completely inadequate sustenance. Those who were not able to work, because of exhaustion or disease, were shot.

With the approach of the Red Army, the *Nyilas*[Arrow Cross] and their SS friends went on a rampage. Hundreds of labor ser-vicemen were killed in cold blood. After the liberation, for ex-ample, the bodies of 790 labor servicemen were exhumed from a mass grave at Hidegseg, about 400 at Ilkamajor, 814 at Nagycenk,

---

[49] Miklós Radnóti, *Forced March: Selected Poems*. Translated from the Hungarian by Clive Wilmer and George Gomori (London: Enitharmon Press, 2003), 86.

350 at Sopron-Banfalva, 300 at Mosonszentmiklos, and 220 near Hegyeshalom. At Köszeg, the labor servicemen were even gassed.[50] These gassings were carried out in sealed barracks by special German commandos. "The surviving labor servicemen were driven toward the Third Reich. Many ended up first in the Mauthausen concentration camp and then in the Gunskirchen camp."[51] Having probably passed along the Köszég-Moson- Sopron route to reach the Nagy-Czenk camp in January 1944, my father was then marched, around November 1944, to the main camp at Mauthausen, in Austria. In January 1945 he was again transferred, this time to the satellite Mauthausen-Gunskirchen camp.

The main Mauthausen camp, focus of a complex of more than four dozen labor camps, was located about twenty kilometers east of the city of Linz, close to the Danube River. Gunskirchen lay south-west of Linz, at a distance of about forty kilometers.

One difficulty of getting a clear and more -or-less complete picture of what happened to my father is that most of the reports of forced marches from Budapest to Mauthausen record these marches as taking place in the fall of 1944 and spring, especially April, 1945. I don't know why my father had done part of this march - from Budapest to Nagy-Czenk- earlier, in January 1944. it may have been because by January 1944 it was already apparent to the Germans that the war was not going in their favor and that defensive works had to be built up urgently. In any case, he was among those who continued the march from the Sopron area (which included Nagy-Czenk) to Mauthausen in the fall of 1944. The marches to Mauthausen seem to have followed two routes: (i) Hartberg-Graz-Bruck-Leoben-Eisenerz-Hieflau-St.Gallen-Steyr- Enns, or (ii) Koszeg-Rechnitz-Strem.and then over to Graz and Bruck. Both ways went through Austrian Alps: the Fischbacheralpen, the Eisenerzeralpen, the Sengsengebirge. Climbing through these high elevations in fall and

---

[50] Braham, *Labor Service*,74.
[51] Ibid.

winter, under the cruel supervision of Waffen- SS companies and malicious local folk, can scarcely be imagined. Court records (in April 1946 a court in Graz examined these war crimes) show that many died of cold and starvation along the way; many were beaten and had their heads smashed or were shot to death. Gold was removed from the teeth of corpses, which were then removed and buried in mass graves by other prisoners[52] The bodies were later discovered, exhumed and re-buried (in one case in the Jewish cemetery at Eisenstadt) at the order of Soviet commanders. The records also show that local villagers spat upon the Jewish slave laborers who were dragging themselves along, as well as political prisoners who followed the same route. The marches took fifteen to twenty days each, and it is estimated that 10,000 Hungarian Jews were driven along in this manner.[53] Out of any given group of 4500, only 100 would arrive at the destination of Mauthausen (called "Mordhausen" by the SS). Beyond those who arrived there on foot, certain contingents were brought by train, especially in April 1945 as the total collapse of the German war effort neared. Between 1938 and 1945, 200,000 prisoners are thought to have passed through the Mauthausen system; between April 1944 and May 1945 there were about 32,000 Jewish prisoners, either in the main camp or in one of the sub-camps.[54] The main camp also contained important political prisoners, such as the former Hungarian Prime Minister Miklós Kallay; Mario Badoglio, son of the Italian Prime Minister; and, as already mentioned, the son of Regent Miklós Horthy. When the Soviets drew closer the younger Horthy and several other important political prisoners, including Leon Blum and Martin Niemöller,

---

[52] Szabolcs Szita, *Verschleppt, Verhungert, Vernichtet: Die Deportation von ungarischen Juden* (Wien: Werner Eichbauer Verlag, 1999), 226.

[53] Ibid.,227.

[54] Hans Marsalek und Kurt Hacker, *Das Konzentrationslager Mauthausen: Nationalsozialistische Konzentrations lager Mauthausen, Gusen, Ebensee und Melk* (Wien: Edition Mauthausen, n.d.), 27.

were moved first to Dachau, near Munich, and then to the Südtirol; from there they were liberated by the U.S. Fifth Army.

Between November 1944 and January 1945, then, my father was in the main camp at Mauthausen. The plateau on which it sat and the entire area is of fairytale beauty. The green -glass Danube flows quietly by, vineyards slumber placidly in sunshine, and little inns with immaculate gardens dot the gently-sloping riverbanks. In spring, when I visited, the air was incredibly gentle, sweet, fresh; grotesquely, it reminded me of the distinctive air in Hebron, in the West Bank, one of Judaism's most holy sites. Indeed, I couldn't comprehend why anyone, including a Nazi, would want to construct such a hideous fortress and place of torture in such a beautiful land-scape. Albert Speer had chosen the location and Heinrich Himmler and Hitler himself made repeated visits over the years.[55]

While there may be an ideological explanation for the choice of locations for concentration camps (it has been suggested that places of exceptional beauty were purposely selected, as somehow underscoring high periods of German cultural or political history), there were often very practical reasons for any given choice. This is certainly true in the cases of Mauthausen and, as is well known, Auschwitz. Mauthausen main camp and many of its satellites are found near stone and marble quarries. These were of vital impor-tance to the National Socialists for several reasons. First, Albert Speer, Hitler's friend charged with grandiose architectural projects in Berlin and Nuremberg, and as of 1942 Minister for Armaments, wanted ready access to stone and marble for the reconstruction of nearby Linz as Hitler's Austrian capital. As early as 1938 Speer had signed a ten-year contract with the *Deutsche Erd -und Steinwerke GmbH*, formed that year, to deliver needed materials.[56] Second, and this became more important as the war went on, large quantities of

---

[55] Hans Marsalek, *Die Geschichte des Konzentrationslagers Mauthausen: Dokumentation* (Wien: Edition Mauthausen, 2000), 12.

[56] Marsalek und Hacker, *Das Konzentrationslager*, 8.

stone were needed for various fortification works. Finally, since the Germans had air supremacy over this area (including the cities of Linz, Steyr, Wels and St. Valentin), it could also be, and was increasingly, used for weapons production: airplanes and metal production, aircraft repair works, tanks and finally rockets.[57] After April 1943, that is to say, after the defeat at Stalingrad, Speer ordered that all forced labor be directed toward armaments and related functions for the war effort.[58]

The daily routine of Mauthausen resembled that of the other major death camps and concentration camps: early morning roll call; twelve or more hours of grinding, heavy labor every day; utterly inadequate food and clothing; overfilled and filthy sleeping quarters; severe beatings and humiliations of every kind; a gas chamber and a crematorium. But it was also somewhat different in the labor that was demanded. The main activity consisted in first, building a staircase leading from the plateau with its various buildings down to floor of the nearby stone quarry, perhaps about one hundred feet down. This staircase was named derisively by the SS as the "Spanish Steps" and the quarry itself the "Wiener Graben." The latter was both an ironic reference to one of Vienna's most important and fashionable streets, and the fact that the quarry had originally been owned by the City of Vienna and had provided paving stones for it. Early every morning the prisoners had to go down the steps (once the staircase was built); spend about eleven hours hacking stone, sometimes for no immediately useful purpose; and go back up the staircase at the end of the day with heavy blocks of stone on their backs (as large as one hundred and ten-pound blocks). Needless to say, this was beyond the physical powers of many. My father, who must have been exceptionally strong, was able to do this. As he quietly mentioned once, he was also able surreptitiously to help some men who were too

---

[57] Marsalek, *Geschichte*, 19.

[58] Ibid., 19, 21.

weak. This went on until he was moved, in mid-March or possibly in mid-April 1945, to the satellite camp at Gunskirchen.

Gunskirchen

On 16 April 1945 about 5,000 men, mainly of Hungarian Jewish origin and of a professional or intellectual background of some sort, were marched from the Mauthausen main camp to Gunskirchen. The main camp had long been over-filled, and aerial bombardments were becoming more frequent, endangering both the SS guards and the laborers. The march covered a distance of about fifty-five kilometers and took three and a half days. In the first few kilometers, toward the bridge over the Danube, about 800 men –already severely undernourished, overworked and exhausted – died. As in every other forced march, those who could not move themselves forward were shot on the spot or simply left to die. Occasionally, in one village or another along the route, villagers would try to toss food to the prisoners, but were warned off by the SS. A few prisoners tried to make a break to the water fountains in town squares, but they were shot immediately. Altogether, in the course of all marches to Gunskirchen, 6,000 persons perished, including women and children. [59]

The construction and settlement of Gunskirchen had begun in December 1944, and was not complete by April 1945. The camp consisted of thirteen very cramped barrack buildings in a wooded area. It lacked almost everything, including any drinking water tanks or lines. By mid-April the camp contained about 2,000 prisoners; typhoid, intestinal diseases, and all kinds of other diseases were rampant. It was the intention of the SS that these prisoners starve to death.[60]

"The penned-in, terrorized masses found no restorative sleep

[59] Szita, *Verschleppt*, 231.

[60] Ibid., 232.

in the half-completed barracks. This inferno further demoralized a number of the prisoners who had been tortured and humiliated for months. In the endless, pitch-dark nights, lying on damp earth, some became apathetic, others began to scream and fell into fits of rage. Some were constantly hallucinating, and there were some who were willing to kill for a piece of bread."[61]

In the early days of May 1945, although German forces continued fighting, sounds of the American advance under General Patton began to be heard. The SS contingent at Mauthausen changed into civilian clothing, put together a "welcoming committee" with a white flag, and was there to meet the 11th Tank Division of the U.S. Third Army on the evening of 4 May. The next day, on 5 May, the 71st Infantry Division completed the liberation of all the camps in the area: Mauthausen, Gunskirchen, Gusen I and II, Linz I and III and others. My father was among those liberated. The commander of the 71st Infantry Division described the event at some length. Here are some extracts from his report:

"Driving up to the camp in our jeep, Cpl. De Spain and I, first knew we were approaching the camp by the hundreds of starving, half-crazed inmates lining the roads, begging for food and cigarettes. Many of them had been able to get only a few hundred yards from the gate before they keeled over and died. As weak as they were, the chance to be free, the opportunity to escape was so great they couldn't resist, though it meant staggering only a few yards before death came. Then came the next indication of the camp's nearness- the smell. There was something about the smell of Gunskirchen I shall never forget. It was strong, yes, and permeating, too. Some six hours after we left the place, six hours spent riding in a jeep, where the wind was whistling around us, we could still detect the Gunskirchen smell. It had permeated our clothing and stayed with us.

---

[61] Ibid.

Of all the horrors of the place, the smell, perhaps, was the most startling of all. It was a smell made up of all kinds of odors- human excreta, foul bodily odors, smoldering trash fires, German tobacco- which is a stink in itself- all mixed together in a heavy dank atmosphere, in a thick, muddy woods, where little breeze could go. The ground was pulpy throughout the camp, churned to a consistency of warm putty by the milling of thousands of feet, mud mixed with feces and urine. The smell of Gunskirchen nauseated many of the Americans who went there.

… It is not an exaggeration to say that almost every inmate was insane with hunger. Just the sight of an American brought cheers, groans and shrieks…The people who couldn't walk crawled out toward our jeep. Those who couldn't even crawl propped themselves upon an elbow…

Sometimes, my guide [an English-speaking prisoner] said, it was so crowded in the buildings that people slept three-deep on the floor, one on top of the other. Often, a man would awake in the morning and find the person under him dead. Too weak to move even the pathetically light bodies of their comrades, the living continued sleeping on them.

I want to make it clear that human beings subjected to the treatment these people were given by the Germans results in a return to the primitive. Dire hunger does strange things. The inmates of Gunskirchen were a select group of prisoners- the intellectual class of Hungarian Jews, for the most part professional people., many distinguished doctors, lawyers, representatives of every skilled field. Yet these people…had been reduced to animals by the treatment of the Germans."[62]

My father's abilities in English may have led to his becoming one of those accompanying the American soldiers in their inspection of

---

[62] The report in the original English may be found on the website of the *Jewish Virtual Library*, under "Gunskirchen." A somewhat shorter, German version is given in Szita, *Verschleppt*,233.

Gunskirchen and setting the processes of provisioning in motion. Within a few days, a water and food supply was arranged; some of the prisoners were transported to nearby hospitals; and German prisoners of war and civilians were set to cleaning up the camp. By 22 June 1945, my father had become a member of the staff of the International Committee of the Red Cross, based in Linz, charged with locating and registering displaced persons "of all nations with the exception of Germans and Austrians," as his identification card states. He traveled about by car. He continued in this role through July and August. The picture on the ICRC identification card shows a young man, somewhat pale, thinner than before but surprisingly well-groomed, in a decent jacket and tie. (Where and how did he obtain these? Perhaps from a small wage paid by the ICRC?) But the eyes– a beautiful grey - and the hesitant, very slight, smile, seem to me to conceal an infinity of wordless pain.

After a lifetime of reflecting on these events, I have concluded that there is no cogent meaning to them. Some people, either having little feeling for the relevance of the past, or lacking ruminative tendencies, will find that glaringly obvious. I don't think it is. Great energies have been expended on constructing philosophies of history, that is, discernible patterns and directions in human history, and to learning from the past. From the Hebrew Bible to Herodotus and Thucydides (*The Pelopponesian War,* which contains its own horrors), through Machiavelli, Hegel and Marx; those living the *vita contemplativa* and those immersed in the *vita activa*; those who are religious and those bent on stamping out religion; all have thought about this question of meaning of historical events. In the immediate case there is the "lesson" that Captain Pletcher from the 71st Infantry Division and author of the report cited above, drew, namely that extreme hunger, deprivation of every kind, torture and humiliation will reduce even intellectuals and highly civilized human beings to crazed, purely physical creatures ready to do one another in for a morsel. But another "lesson" is a demonstration of the fact

of human resilience. Many of those who survived Mauthausen and
Gunskirchen, and of course the other death and labor camps, were
subsequently able to build fruitful, constructive lives. According to
my father, there was an element of willpower. He spoke of a moment
in the quarry at Mauthausen when he resolved not to let the SS crush
him. This brings to my mind the philosopher Hegel's master-slave
dialectic, with the slave refusing the recognition the master craves,
and, over the longer term, "winning." Such moments of resolution or
decision were also later made an important element in the psychologist Viktor Frankl's interpretation of the Holocaust and his later
"logotherapy." Frankl was from a Viennese Jewish background and
also incarcerated at Mauthausen. Nonetheless, whatever the merits
of his theories, I find the argument and tone of his well-known work
Man's Search for Meaning (1946) a little too lacking in understanding
for those who had lost any will to live. In any event, while for my
father it seemed to have been a critical moment, it may also have
been a fleeting emotion and perhaps unknown providential forces
were at work in his ultimate survival.

Mother

Szatmárnémeti Before the War

Some portions of a room draped in nighttime darkness will appear slightly less obscure than others. While the lives of my paternal grandparents disappeared into near-total oblivion, some pictures, documents and letters regarding my mother's family remain in existence. I rely partly on these, and partly on my mother's own limited statements, to reconstruct her experience of life in and deportation from Szatmár, Transylvania.

Today, as I mentioned in the Preface, the name 'Szatmár' encapsulates a special history and legacy of what has been termed "Extreme Orthodoxy."[63] The county of Szatmár, and its main city of Szatmárnémeti, is a neighbor of Maramaros county in northeastern Hungary, in the Carpathian foothills. This is where the Satmar religious movement began. A contemporary scholar of this history has written:

"From an historical perspective we can conclude that the two rabbinical figures and ideologies that had the greatest impact on the relationship between Extreme Orthodoxy and the rest of the Jewish world after the Holocaust originated from what might be called "the Maramaros legacy." Through the activities of Rabbi Yosef Zvi

---

[63] Menachem Keren-Kratz, "Maramaros, Hungary: The Cradle of Extreme Orthodoxy," *Modern Judaism*, Vol.35, No.2, 2015, 168.

Dushinsky and Rabbi Yoel Teitelbaum, Extreme Orthodoxy established a generally recognized leadership, distinct organizations, be-
havioral characteristics, canonic texts and even segregated residential
spheres. ...[E]ach in his own way contributed to the transformation
of Extreme Orthodoxy from a disorganized sporadic social-religious
phenomenon in 1860s Hungary into a fully-fledged religious movement in 1960s Israel and the U.S."[64]

The Yoel Teitelbaum referred to here was a descendant of Yosef
Teitelbaum (1758-1841) and of Rabbi Moshe Sofer, the *Hatam Sofer*
(1762-1839), both of whose writings formed the core of the movement based in Maramaros county. Jews had settled in the area after the Khmelnytsky pogroms (1648-49) in the Polish-Lithuanian
Commonwealth. Being close to the southern Polish region of Galicia,
the Jewish community in Maramaros also received visits from the
Baal Shem Tov (1700-1760), founder of Hasidism. For various reasons relating to both family and ideological disputes, in 1905 Yoel
Teitelbaum traveled slightly southwest from Sighet, long a Hasidic
seat within Maramaros county, to settle and found a community
in Szatmár.

The Hasidic community in Szatmár, however, formed only a
part of the Jewish community. Many of Szatmár's Jews belonged, by
the end of the nineteenth century, either to the more liberal Neolog
or to the Status Quo movements (corresponding very roughly to
what in American terms would be Reform and Conservative congregations). Both of my mother's parents, Rozsa Reiter and Samuel
Fekete, descended from lines of Neolog and Status Quo inhabitants
of Szatmárnémeti or nearby towns; their graves are to be seen today
in the Neolog cemetery. Rozsi Reiter (1887-1944) was the daughter of Jakab Reiter from Szatmár, and Leora Adler from Kassa.
Samu Fekete was born in 1877 into the Schwartz family in Szatmár.
"Fekete" is the Magyarized form of "Schwartz". It is possible that the

---

[64] Ibid.

Schwartz family were originally from the Burgenland (a German-speaking border area between Hungary and Austria), but I have no information on that. Samu's parents, Albert Schwartz and Regina Krausz, had six other children: Jozsef (b.1873), Riza (b.1875), Dezsö (1878), Laura Lina (b.1880), Antal Toni (b.1882), Juliska (b. 1886). My mother never mentioned any of these aunts and uncles except Dezsö, with whom she later became quite close. At least two of them died young; the others died during deportation or at Auschwitz.

Samu studied medicine and ophthalmology in Budapest, Dresden and Berlin. His first appointments were at the Budapest Ophthalmology Clinic and Szent István Hospital. In 1904 he returned to Szatmár, and during World War I he served in the 12th Infantry Regiment of the Hungarian Army, as the regimental doctor. He was posted to the Russian Front, and was decorated for his service. After the war, Samu became chief physician for a work-insurance company in Szatmár. He was active in both scientific and professional matters, becoming president of the Szatmár County Physicians' Chamber; he was also active in the local Status Quo congregation.

In 1909 Samu married Rozsi Reiter, and they had two daughters: Zsuzsa, born in May 1912, and my mother Katalin (Kato), born in October 1914. There is a report that Samu and Rozsi also had a foster child -Jenö Fekete -but again, my mother never mentioned this. Whoever he was, it is most likely that he, too, died while in the labor service system or as a result of deportation.

The 1920s saw a considerable amount of activity in Szatmárnémeti in regard to Jewish community life as well as Zionism.[65] Various organizations were formed to improve conditions for the poorer classes: the Orphans' Dressmaker's Shop; the Jewish Craftsman Apprentice School; and a bank for low-income Jews. In addition, planning began for a Jewish hospital, which could pay adequate

---

[65] Csirak Csaba and Gyuri Elefant, *Szatmar Jews in the Service of Health* (Szatmárnémeti 2012), 2.

attention to Jewish needs and practices, and which would employ Jewish staff. State-run hospitals in Szatmár County, at this point under Romanian rule, did not employ many, if any, Jewish doctors, nurses or mid-wives.[66] Accordingly, in about 1927, the Orthodox and Status Quo congregations agreed to cooperate in the founding of a hospital. After years of negotiations and constructions delays, the hospital (*Beit Hacholim Haivri*) opened on 25 September 1937. Dr. Samu Fekete was appointed chief physician. A journalist, writing for the newspaper *Roggeli Ujsag* the following year, described the significance of the hospital's opening as follows:

"Let's stop for a minute at the door of a ten-bed ward where issues like wealth, majority and minority, racism and world politics cease to exist. There are mere people here, and prayers, in whatever language [Hungarian, Yiddish, Romanian, German] they might be said, all sound the same: "God help me, please!"[67]

One of the earliest patients was the young Elie Wiesel from Maramaróssighet (Sighet), who came in with appendicitis. The future Nobel Peace Prize winner was enchanted with the hospital, and especially one of the nurses.[68]

Such achievements notwithstanding, the lives and fates of the Jews of Szatmár and Northern Transylvania turned out to be far from a simple progression. The tranquil, orderly sequences of life under the Hapsburg Empire, described, for example, in Joseph Roth's *Radetzkymarsch*, had disappeared in 1918, along with the Austro-Hungarian Empire itself.

Like Germany, Russia, and Ukraine, with the collapse of empire Hungary experienced a brutal civil war in 1919. Conservative forces tried to undo the communist revolutions, with varying success. In Hungary this meant that "white" forces led by Miklós Horthy sought

---

[66] Ibid.,7.

[67] Ibid., 6.

[68] Elie Wiesel, *All Rivers Run to the Sea*: *Memoirs* (New York: Alfred A. Knopf, 1995), 25.

to take back power from the "red" workers' movements headed by Béla Kun (Kohn), a Transylvanian Jew. In conjunction with the counter-revolutionary effort, which was successful in Hungary and ultimately in Germany as well (but obviously not in the new Soviet Union), Hungary was the first country to establish anti-Jewish laws and policies. The Minorities' Treaty of 1923, which was part of a sequence of peace treaties signed at Versailles after World War I, was supposed to guarantee civil rights and civic equality to national minorities, but in the case of Hungarian Jews it proved to be largely ineffective. Although most of the Jews of Hungary and Transylvania did not realize it, the gains toward emancipation which had been made in the previous century were on the way to be being completely undermined.[69] The first anti-Jewish measure, passed in 1920, related to the proportion of Jews allowed in institutions of higher education. This was the *numerus clausus*," limiting Jewish participation to 6 percent, down from percentages sometimes as high as 50 percent, depending on the field and place of study. Later, other areas of social, cultural and political life were also targeted, closely resembling the Nuremberg Laws in Germany (1935-1938). The First Anti-Jewish Law, passed in May 1938, required the removal of Jews from intellectual occupations such as those in academic institutions, journalism, theaters, the legal and medical professions, and so on; it prohibited Jewish persons from serving in the civil service and other areas of civic and economic life. The Second Anti-Jewish Law (May 1939) set up various categories and degrees of Jewishness, depending on how many grandparents were Jewish. This law also limited Jews' participation in the Hungarian military and provided the legal basis for the establishment of the labor service system. The Third Anti-Jewish Law (1941) forbade intermarriage between Jews and non-Jews. Yet another law, passed in March 1942, banned Jews

---

[69] Guy Miron, *The Waning of Emancipation: Jewish History, Memory, and the Rise of Fascism in Germany, France, and Hungary* (Detroit: Wayne State University Press, 2011), Ch.5.

from being employed in public medical institutions and pharmacies without a special exemption. Jews could not go to public swimming pools, steam baths or other such recreational facilities. All of this meant that Jews in Hungary were almost entirely excluded from economic and social life, and had no means of earning a living.

I described the nature of the Hungarian labor-service system above. After 1942, Jewish doctors in Hungary were drafted into this service. Some of them were drawn from public hospitals such as the Szatmárnémeti Royal State Hospital. Any income derived from remaining Jews registered as employees of such hospitals had to be turned over to the local Medical Association (presumably including now only non-Jews).[70] This was a further humiliation, and a further effort to remove the means of subsistence from Jews and their families.

Complicating the situation of Hungarian -speaking Jews still further was the back-and-forth between Hungary, Russia and Romania about various territories, mainly Transylvania, Bukovina, and Bessarabia. We have already seen that as a result of the Trianon Treaty of 1920, rule over Transylvania had been transferred from Hungary to Romania. Romania enacted its own anti-Jewish legislation, and, as is well known, tolerated even more viciously antisemitic attitudes among the general population than was the case in Hungary. In many places, including Szatmár, a vigorous effort at Romanization was undertaken, with the Romanian language being required in schools and other public institutions. Again, as we saw in the previous section, the Second Vienna Award in August 1940 returned Northern Transylvania, including Szatmár, to Hungary. In this way the Jews of Northern Transylvania became subject to Hungarian government policy, and all that that later entailed.

My mother, Kató, was enrolled in a convent school in Szatmár, in which the Hungarian-speaking girls would have had some

---

[70] Csirak and Elefant, *Szatmar Jews*, 7.

instruction in Romanian as well. Although she did not mention it, it is likely that the Jewish girls in the school experienced some forms of antisemitic prejudice or harassment. This was certainly the case ten or twelve years later, when her second cousin, Livia Reiter (younger daughter of Viktor Reiter, who gave my father a job in his sugar factory) attended the school.[71] At the age of fifteen or sixteen, that is, in about 1930, Kató spent some weeks in Palestine with a youth group of some sort, learning about Zionism. She remained a quiet supporter of Israel throughout her life, while sometimes conveying an astonishing -to me–understanding for Palestinian Arab resistance. She later spent a year at what used to be called a "finishing school" in Vienna, where she improved her German and acquired an intense, lifelong admiration for Viennese, and more broadly western European, culture.

As the economic and political situation of the Jews in Hungary deteriorated in the late 1930s, Samu became increasingly afraid that Kató might be left to fend for herself. Her beautiful older sister Zsuzsa had married an architect, Zoltan Boros, and had a small son, Janos, in the early 1940s. In photographs, Zoltan appears very handsome, blond and athletic, fun-loving. Perhaps coming under some parental pressure, and after what seems to have been a fairly normal, busy, social life with parties, ski-trips in the Carpathians, and coffees at Budapest's elegant Gerbeaud coffee house, my mother married a Budapest lawyer, Pál Janos Adonyi. Pál Janos was born in Zemplen County in 1903, the son of Gyula Adonyi and Karolina Zsurger. He was some eleven years older than my mother, and well-established. The newly-married couple resided in an apartment on Erzsébet Square 13, in Budapest's VII. District. The date of this marriage is rather mysterious, though my mother certainly told me about it. I would guess that it took place in either 1940 or 1941. A marriage certificate in my possession seems quite spurious: the date

---

[71] Personal communication, August 2020.

on this certificate is first given as 15 June 1944, but this is then crossed out and changed to 27 June. But by this time my mother was in Auschwitz and Pál Janos would have been known to be either still in the labor-service system somewhere, or, more likely, dead. One of the witnesses listed on this certificate was Samu's brother Dezsö, also a lawyer living in Budapest. I surmise that it was he who arranged in some way to have this certificate created, so as to confirm a marriage and property ownership that had been in existence. He may have hoped–having, like many people, a rather vague idea of where Jews were being deported to-- that either his niece or her husband might someday return and would need to be able to claim their property. Other than for this reason, I cannot think why he would have done it, if he did. The certificate also states that the bride's citizenship "could not be ascertained," and that the bride "refused to adhere" to Government Order 4908. I have not been able to discover what this Government Order contained. The reference to citizenship is a reference to the Anti-Jewish Laws and the political debates around them: the citizenship of Jews whose families had inhabited Hungary for hundreds of years was now denied, and this could only be disputed or rectified by special procedures or exemptions.

German Invasion of Hungary and Planning for Jewish Destruction

I turn now to the time leading up to May 1944, when the Jews of Szatmár were deported to Auschwitz. I will first give an overview which relies on historical sources, and then bring in a loose collection of letters written during this period by Samu. These letters were kept by my mother for more than sixty years, in no particular order, in an old manila envelope. She never mentioned them, or their possible significance to anyone but herself. Since having them translated long after her death in 2010, I have come to realize that they give a useful and, of course, to me very moving account of this time of persecution, ghettoization, and deportation, as well as an unexpected glimpse into my grandfather's personality.

The Germans invaded Hungary on 19 March 1944.[72] For years, Hungarians had believed that they would be able to avoid this calamity and remain more or less secure through their contribution to Hitler's war in the East, through trade, and through the indirect pressure of the 1938 Bled Agreement with the Little Entente. The alliance called the Little Entente had been formed in 1921 among Czechoslovakia, Romania and Yugoslavia. The aim had been to deter potential Hungarian revanchism arising from the Trianon Treaty; it was intended to ensure that Hungary would not re-arm after World War I. In August 1938, however, at a meeting in Bled, Yugoslavia, some of the restrictions on Hungary were lifted, including restrictions on rearmament, and assurances were given concerning mutual non-aggression by the four nations involved. Thus Hungary's overall position, and therefore its position with respect to Germany, was somewhat strengthened.

At the same time, that is during the inter-war period, many in the Jewish community believed that their historically quite good relations with the governing conservative aristocracy, as well as their contributions to Hungarian society since the Compromise of 1867, would generally protect them. But German political pressure on Hungary steadily increased. On 20 November 1940 Hungary joined the Tripartite Pact (originally between Germany, Italy and Japan); in June 1941 it participated in the German invasion of the Soviet Union; in December 1941 it formally declared war on Great Britain and the United States. In at least one meeting between Hitler, Horthy, von Ribbentrop and the Hungarian Foreign Minister Döme Sztójay, in April 1943, it became clear to the Hungarians, if it had not already been so, that "sooner or later a positive German intervention in the

---

[72] Cf. above, 33.

problem of the position of Jewry in Hungary must be expected."[73] Meanwhile, German economic control in Hungary had also significantly increased. By 1944, the Dresdener Bank had direct control of 16 percent of the Hungarian Credit Bank of Budapest, and German companies had obtained increased control over vital oil, bauxite and timber resources.[74] The I.G. Farben Chemical Company also had substantial interests here. Thus the ultimate reasons for the German invasion of Hungary were various and many, in a critical context of impending total defeat.[75]

On 20 March 1944, the day after the invasion, which had only involved a relatively small contingent of SS and a somewhat larger Wehrmacht force, Adolf Eichmann's *Sondereinsatzkommando für Judenvernichtung* (Special Force for Destruction of Jews) also entered the country. Eichmann, staying first at the Astoria Hotel and then taking over a beautiful villa (formerly belonging to a Jewish businessman) in the Svábhegy neighborhood of Budapest, immediately began planning the "de-Jewification" of the country. The Gestapo (short for *Geheime Staatspolizei)*, led by Dieter Wisliçeny, established itself initially in the historic Rabbinical Seminary in the VIII. District; that building soon became a detention center for Jews and a transit camp to deportation. Shortly afterwards the Gestapo transferred its main operations to Sip Street in central Pest. Charging the cost of supplies and requisitions to the Jewish community, the Gestapo installed itself in the large building which had housed the main offices of the very large Neolog Jewish community before the war, and during the war became the seat of the Central Jewish

---

[73] Jeno Levai, *Black Book on the Martyrdom of Hungarian Jewry.* Edited by Lawrence P. Davis (Zurich: Central European Times Publishing Co., Ltd, 1948), 33.

[74] Fenyo, *Hitler, Horthy,* 83.

[75] Cf. above, 18.

Committee.[76] The seat of the Orthodox community on Dob Street was converted for similar purposes.

Eventually the principal German SS officers, Adolf Eichmann, Dieter Wisliçeny, Hermann Krumey, and others, and their staffs, settled their headquarters in some pleasant buildings in Svábhegy, where there were some of the green spaces that they sought. The buildings in question were being used as holiday homes and sanitoria. When the SS decided to move in, within minutes the Jewish residents were driven straight to a detention center; the others were simply thrown out and left to fend for themselves. Again in short order, Regent Horthy appointed a new government headed by Döme Sztójay, formerly Foreign Minister. Under the influence of the SS, who had done this many times before (and were not hesitant to trumpet their professional experience), the Sztójay government quickly began to ensure that German aims would be fulfilled. A spate of anti-Jewish measures was announced, notably the requirement that all Jews wear a yellow star on their outer clothing, and the expropriation of whatever personal and commercial property they might still have retained. At a meeting in the Ministry of the Interior on the 4 April 1944, a plan was worked out for the ghettoization and deportation of all Hungarian Jews. The plan was put together between Eichmann's *Sonderkommando* and various Hungarian government representatives, including László Baky, László Endre and Andor Jaross. Also involved was the liaison officer of the Hungarian Gendarmerie to the Gestapo, Lieutenant-Colonel László Ferenczy. Ferenczy would turn out to be one of the most energetic and vicious of the war criminals involved in the destruction of Hungarian Jews. That is, until it became even clearer, in the fall of 1944, that Germany was going to lose the war. At that point he changed sides

---

[76] Erno Munkacsi, *How It Happened: Documenting the Tragedy of Hungarian Jewry.*Translated from the Hungarian by Peter Baliko Lengyes. Edited by Nina Munk. Annotated by Lazlo Csosz and Ferenc Laczo (Montreal: McGill-Queens University Press, 2018), 33-36.

and sought to co-operate with a notional resistance movement in Budapest. First, however, Ferenczy set up a Hungarian counterpart to Eichmann's *Sonderkommando*. It was called the "Hungarian Squad for the Extermination of the Jews," and was headquartered on Semmelweis Street in Budapest, not far from the office of Ferenczy's supervisor, Laszlo Endre, sub-prefect of Pest. The sign outside the buiding read: "International Storage and Transport Company."[77] (Endre shortly became state secretary in the Ministry of the Interior, with offices in the Castle District of Buda.)

Although not formally published until 26 April as a government decree, the "de-Jewification" plan was practically in effect after 7 April, by means of a secret decree signed by Baky. On 12 April the government declared Northern Transylvania and Carpatho-Ruthenia a military operational zone, retroactive to 1 April. This meant, of course, that many illegitimate measures could be undertaken in the name of military security.

The ghettoization and deportation plan was organized into roughly four stages: 1) Jews in rural areas and small towns were to be collected in community buildings, such as synagogues, and their valuables confiscated. 2) Transfer of these Jews to ghettos in larger towns in their region, often the county seat. Thus the city of Szatmárnémeti, seat of Szatmár county, was the location of a major ghetto to which Jews from smaller towns were transferred. 3) Setting up of ghettos in the larger cities and towns. The ghettos had to be completely cut off from the rest of the city and established either in the already-existing Jewish quarter, or in brickyards (a preferred location because of the actual need for bricks and the work associated with that), warehouses and/or factories. Where these were not available or insufficient, a field under open sky could also be used. 4) "Loading" of Jews onto trains and deportation to concentration and death camps. To facilitate the entire process, the country was

---

[77] Levai, *Black Book*, 115. See also Munkacsi, *How It Happened*, 185.

divided into six operational zones, corresponding to one or more already-existing Gendarmerie districts, of which there nine. Szatmár in Northern Transylvania belonged to Gendarmerie District IX; other parts of Transylvania, such as Maramaros County, mentioned above, belonged to districts VIII and X.[78] A sequence for deportation was also drawn up.

Further planning sessions for specific Gendarmerie districts took place in late April. The meeting concerning Szatmár County and neighboring cities such as Nagybánya (seat of the Horthy family) took place in the city of Szatmárnémeti itself on 26 April.In addition to László Endre from the Ministry of the Interior, the attendees were important local officials such as mayors of larger towns, and their assistants; chiefs of the regional and local Gendarmerie and police forces; and regional prefects or deputy prefects. László Ferenczy was present, as was a representative from the Ministry of Supply. It was announced that the local Jewish Council would be responsible for establishing the ghetto; the Council members would have to provide for public health in the form of sanitation, water, and medical care, as well as ensuring that money and valuables- -which were now to be considered "property of the state"–were promptly and fully turned over to the police or Gendarmerie. How the Council members were supposed to do all this, having themselves undergone a decade of increasing impoverishment and powerlessness, was left undiscussed. From this planning meeting, nonetheless, there followed, for Northern Transylvania, "the most ruthless and concentrated process of destruction of the war."[79]

---

[78] Christian Gerlach, Götz Aly, *Das letzte Kapitel: Der Mord an den ungarischen Juden 1944-1945* (Frankfurt am Main: Fischer Taschenbuch Verlag, 2004), Ch.5.

[79] Braham, *Genocide*, 16,18.

The Fekete Family 1942-1944

Pál Janos Adonyi, my mother's first husband, was recruited into the labor-service system, along with all other Hungarian Jewish males between the ages of twenty and forty-eight, in April 1942 (a family letter refers to the date of his recruitment as 22 April). From then on, my mother seems to have divided her time between Budapest and her parents' home in Szatmár. As conditions for Jews grew worse, especially after March 1944, it might have been safer for her to remain in Budapest and try to hide there, as hundreds of Jews did. But for various reasons she chose not to. As she told me, in very sparing terms, she could not support the idea of abandoning her family in such circumstances. Unfortunately she did not specify what she had understood to be the circumstances. It does not seem to me that she, any more than anyone else living in provincial Hungary, had any definite conception of what was going on in Auschwitz and elsewhere, and what exactly deportation entailed. In any case she preferred to accept the consequences of a decision to go back to the provinces. Although my mother had probably never read the book of Esther, I can't help thinking of Esther's own reported thoughts, as she prepared a dangerous approach the Persian King on behalf of the Jewish people: "If I perish, I perish."[80]

The letters I possess from my grandfather Samu to his brother Dezsö in Budapest begin around 1940 and end in late April or early May,1944. Some of them are not dated, and I have to guess from the content as to when they were likely to have been written. At no point, including the very last letter concerning ghettoization in Szatmár, was mention made of extermination and "the final solution." The earliest letters recount the tribulations of everyday life under the anti-Jewish restrictions and the pressures of wartime: exorbitant electricity bills, high taxes of various kinds, the departure of a longtime servant (their household, like many upper middle-class

---

[80] *Book of Esther*, Ch.4:16.

households of the time, employed a cook or maid or seamstress, or sometimes all three). My grandfather mentions weakening health - a heart condition- and the difficulty of going out during wintertime. The family also owned a vineyard, somewhere farther out in the countryside; it became urgent to sell this, not only because Jews were no longer permitted to own such property, but because the family needed money.

"I was glad to read that you [Dezsö and family] are all doing well and glad to read your optimistic observations as well, although I don't quite share your hopeful views. Selling of the vineyard is well underway I don't deny that it is somewhat painful to give up this pleasant and dear place, but on the other hand I realize that it is too much for us now. It means work, and sometimes not easy work, under terrible travel circumstances. Even if the law about Jewish holdings did not exist, we would still sell it."[81]

My mother told me that she was convinced that her life was saved in Auschwitz by poor Orthodox women who were grateful to her father for having treated them and their families *gratis* for many years. These women would have managed to give her an extra morsel of food, or perhaps a useful piece of clothing, or would have protected her in some other way. In one letter Samu also refers to the fact of free treatment, but is focused on a concrete return:

"I talked to Miklós Heilbrun, and told him to send his father to me. He was my patient for decades, at no cost. He should bring along a round sheep [goat?] cheese, I will pay good money for it. I am aware of how hard it is to obtain foodstuffs in Pest, and I will help you as much as I can, just send a note. Right now, in our town [Szatmár], draft notices for labor camps are being delivered. Janos sent four postcards already; he only mentions, in one of his letters, that "we are working hard." Otherwise he just writes that he is healthy."

---

[81] Undated letter.

"The Fogarassy vineyard lawsuit had the first hearing this week."[82]

The last sentence quoted seems to be a reference to a family with whom Samu was in dispute over the sale of his vineyard, but I do not know how this matter was resolved, if at all. A letter in the previous month, May 1942, revealed that Dezsö was assisting Samu in a number of other lawsuits in and around Szatmár, apparently trying to prove either that they did not owe certain moneys, or to obtain moneys that they thought were owed to them. There was also an effort to find a legal solution to the citizenship question. Apparently Samu, like many other Hungarian Jews, was no longer considered a citizen, and he was trying to find a way to undo this state of affairs. There is some discussion, in the same May letter, of Samu and Rozsi traveling to Budapest to try to move their legal appeals ahead at the Ministry of the Interior; Samu mentions planning to stay with my mother "in the remaining part of Kató's home."[83] (Presumably my mother had rented out part of her apartment.) But in the end they were not in the mood to travel, as there had not been any further word from Pál Janos. Meanwhile, Rozsi was not only struggling to manage a large house without any help, but was showing emerging signs of memory loss: "I am certain that Rozsi's absentmindedness is not always a common, everyday thing. It is not completely her fault that we have to bear the consequences, but my state of health, and the fact that I am limited in movement, makes it difficult ."[84]

In May,1942, Samu was sixty-five years old, and no longer able to carry on his private medical practice as he would wish, or to go to his club. If I recall correctly, my mother told me that there was a time when he went to the Hotel Dacia every evening to play cards, but that had evidently come to an end:

"I am powerless, lazy, without energy or drive. I am a real

---

[82] Letter from June 1942.
[83] Letter of 13 May 1942.
[84] Letter of 13 May 1942.

Oblomov in this way.[85] I am busy daily until about 5:00pm, and after that I am not able to do anything. It is impossible for me to sit down in the evening to do some work; at 9:00 or 10:00pm I want to go to bed, or maybe voraciously read some stupid novel. In the morning when I get up, around 8:00am, I am already tired I cannot tell you, besides my regular daily duties, how I spend the rest of my time. The club does not exist anymore; the café has a part called "art gallery," that's where the members gather now, but I don't go there anymore. I spend my afternoons alone at home or go to Zsuzska's."[86]

When I saw the Hotel Dacia in 2005, it was a large building on one the main squares of the city, overlooking a park. It was an eerie montage of some sort of grim nineteenth- century architecture (not yellow-colored baroque, as are several of the other principal buildings of the city), with Stalinist- era neon lighting and unused internal guard-posts. The dining room, perhaps formerly a warm place for pastries, coffee and cards, was now a scarcely-populated, cavernous space with red and silver velvety wallpaper and sullen wait staff.

In November 1942, Zoltan and Pál Janos, the two sons-in-law in the labor service system (like my father) were still in communication with Samu, complaining only of the cold. Zoltan was either a Christian or had converted to Christianity, as he seems to have been helped a little in the labor service by the Reformed Church - Church officials arranged a two-day leave for him.[87] The two sisters, Zsuzsa and Kató, spent their time outdoors, bike-riding, planting potatoes, and taking care of Zsuzsa's little son Jani. My mother, Kató, had also become very friendly with my father's family, especially his sister Emmy. I have a postcard from Emmy (written in German in 1940), from Petresti, where she and her husband Feri had gone for a little

[85] Reference to the Russian novel *Oblomov* (1859) by Ivan Goncharov.
[86] Ibid
[87] There was some willingness on the part some pastors to issue certificates of conversion without enquiring too closely as to the sincerity of the applicants. See Hanebrink, *In Defense of Christian Hungary*, 203.

relaxation. It relates a few happy days of sunbathing and conveys kind, warm greetings to all of my mother's family. Kató at some point also traveled to Kis-Sikarlo in central Transylvania; this was the location of her brother-in-law Zoltan's labor service, perhaps also that of her husband, Pál Janos, though that is not known.

By January 1943, Samu decided that "money is no object any more, I have nothing left," so that the expense of a trip to Budapest might as well be undertaken. More important than the money question was the problem of Zsuzsa's health. She was losing a great deal of weight, for no clear reason, and looked very unwell; Samu and his medical colleagues in Szatmár were unable to determine a cause. Samu also thought that his own heart problems could use more specialized attention. Through some connection or other, Samu was able to reserve a room in which to stay at the Institute for Internal Medicine on Stefania Street in Budapest. No letter remains in which the results of this visit are reported, but Zsuzsa lived long enough to be deported to Auschwitz, together with her small son and all the other Jews in the Szatmár ghetto, in May 1944.

By March 1943, Samu found himself increasingly irritated by what he saw as his brother's misplaced optimism about the general situation, and rather sarcastic humor. Dezsö had apparently written to him in a joking manner about the rather small packets of food that Rozsi was sending to him and his wife in Budapest. "I know very well that without these ["Insignificant little packages"] you would be starving. I know your household; not too long ago I was there [referring to the January medical visit] and had the opportunity, together with Zsuzska, to starve with you together."[88] Samu was also concerned because my mother, Kató, seemed to be staying at Dezsö's (in Budapest) for weeks at a time, and there simply was not enough food to go around.

"Write what it is that we have here and could send [you],

---

[88] Letter of 19 March 1943.

considering the difficulties with the post office and the lack of intermediaries. The smartest thing would be if you could send travelers to us who could look us up and help carry the packages. The travelers leaving our town are usually so overwhelmed with their own problems that I cannot persuade them to look you up. I hear that Peter's [Dezsö's son, also in Budapest] luck ran out; it is his turn [to be recruited into the labor service]. But fortunately he is in a tolerable situation [i.e. can probably sleep at home or return home quite frequently]."

"All this just needs to be survived. This is how it is with Zoli [Zoltan, Zsuzsa's husband], too; he works in an engineering job [probably an overstatement] in Sikarlo, so that he can sometimes visit home. Janos's case, so mysterious, worries us endlessly. Hoping every day that the mail will bring something; disappointed every day, again and again, and knowing that Kató goes through the same thing, though she hides it well. But we have to survive this too, as long as necessary.

Another thing to mention: the Ministry of the Interior sent me my citizenship certificate."[89]

The summer of 1943 seems to have brought something of an interlude. At least, there was a complete change of tone in Samu's letters, as he tried to persuade Dezsö to take his vacation in "the old home," Szatmár. He warned against trying other places in the area, such as Nagybánya. Indeed, Nagybánya would, less than a year later, become the location of one of the worst ghettos in Hungary.

"[Don't visit Nagybánya.] They have an auxiliary camp for the Jewish conscripts in the compulsory labor service and they have several hundred, sometimes several thousand, visitors daily .You would not easily find a place to stay or something to eat I would recommend going to Raho. There is a wonderful hotel there, the authorities from the capital [of the country or the county unclear]

[89] Ibid.

built that for its personnel. Kató could tell you more about it, she spent time there last year.

How did we not think of the most obvious place, though, Szatmár! Laura's [their sister's] house is empty and if we still have some obstacles, we have Riza's house, she can stay [somewhere else]. If the Victoria [hotel or restaurant] is not kosher enough for you [he means good enough], there is still the Pannonia I can assure you, you won't starve, even if you don't bring food coupons."[90]

In the end, Dezsö's wife Klari came for an extended stay with Samu and Rozsi during July, and Dezsö came for a shorter time in August, when they returned together to Budapest. The following month, Samu, Rozsi and my mother decided to take their own brief vacation in Budapest "just to live a little bit differently."[91] They stayed at the Hotel Hungaria.

Although Samu had "decided" not to worry any further about money, since he had no more with which to pay various fees for lawsuits and newly-imposed taxes, by December 1943 he was again quite anxious about these matters. In one tax matter in which he had made a written appeal to the local tax office, the appeal was conveniently misplaced, and he was "given the run-around," with one bureaucrat referring him to another, no-one showing any knowledge of the appeal, let alone sympathy. He now suffered continual pain in both hands, such that he found it very difficult either to write by hand or to type. "This whole thing was so trying, for my heart and for my dignity, and it was so hard to climb the stairs [to the tax office], I can't tell you how."[92] Nonetheless it appears that a couple of weeks later the case was resolved in Samu's favor; the tax collection was "suspended." "Nowadays almost daily we face such unpleasantness. For example, our monthly electricity bill, after we

---

[90] Letter of 22 June 1943.
[91] Letter of 24 September 1943.
[92] Letter of 10 December 1943.

used the electric heater for the first time, was 400 pengö; this is not a typographical error. "[93]

Writing again in early January 1944, Samu explains that his moods are very variable, and that the tone of his letter might be entirely different in a different hour. He is again irked by his brother's general optimism and suggestion that he, Samu, has nothing about which to complain. "It is not impossible that there will be a time when the everyday small annoyances will be compensated by small everyday joys, but more likely we should be ready for the opposite."[94] Again it is noteworthy that at this late date Samu appears to have had no inkling of the larger deportation and extermination processes underway for the Jews in other regions of Europe. At least, he never alluded to them.

Ghettoization and Deportation

As stated above, a planning meeting for the "de-Jewification" of Transylavania and other parts of Hungary was held in Szatmár on 26 April,1944. It was put into effect very rapidly. On 3 May the mayor, László Czoka, issued the following statement:

"I inform the Jews living in the territory of the municipality who, in accord with my decree No.12080 …are obliged to wear the distinctive badge, that beginning at 5:00am on 3 May they cannot leave their homes. Those Jews who do not live in the designated quarter –the Jewish camps [ghetto]—may not leave their homes from 4 May until the issuance of new directives, except daily between 9:00am and 11:00am exclusively to acquire drinking water, strictly necessary food, and the essentials for their existence. Those who violate this provision will be interned."[95]

---

[93] Ibid.
[94] Letter of 9 January 1944.
[95] Braham, *Genocide*, 101.

Detailed accounts of the ghetto of Szatmár as well as all other regions of Hungary can be found in the records of the trials conducted by People's Courts in Hungary and Romania after 1945. In Szatmár 18,000-19,000 Jews were moved into and confined to apartment buildings in a certain section of the city, an area that was fit to hold perhaps one twentieth of that number. They came from Szatmár itself as well as from the concentration camps, such as that in Nagyvárad, not far away. There were ten to fifteen people in a room; the food and water supplies were totally and deliberately inadequate. One witness reported:

"Upon entering the ghetto, all the people were subjected to searches [for valuables], and the women were also vaginally searched under shameful conditions. We were compelled to surrender all our valuables to a police or gendarmerie officer.

As far as feeding was concerned, we received so little food from the mayor's office that one could not live on it. Therefore, from funds collected for communal purposes, we once paid [secretary general for the mayor's office]] Counselor [Ernö] Pirkler 200,000 pengö to get us supplies from outside. I must note that he accepted this sum the day before the beginning of the deportation."[96]

Many men and women were subjected to severe torture by Hungarians –police, Gendarmerie and their citizen- informers—in pursuit of gold, jewels, and other valuable items. They were repeatedly beaten on the bare soles of their feet with truncheons and wire, and over their entire bodies, so that they could no longer walk. In their already-weakened condition- -lack of food and water, years of persecution and loss of civil rights, expropriation—they were not able to withstand this.

An acquaintance of my mother's, Anna Molnar Hegedüs (who also eventually settled in Montreal), wrote an account of the Szatmár ghetto in Hungarian soon after the war. Her book was translated

---

[96] Braham, *Genocide*, 102.

into English and published under the title *As the Lilacs Bloomed* in 2014. Samu also briefly described the initial phase of ghettoization in a letter to Dezsö. It seems that several family members, including my mother, had moved into an apartment within the ghetto confines that was owned by Samu's sister Riza. Samu was able to obtain a delay or temporary exemption for himself and Rozsi on the ground of being a physician.

"As far as our inner mood is concerned it [the situation] is impossible and unsustainable, but we still try to maintain our strength in the hope that we can do something for them. ... In the interests of my children I will submit a petition; following the new government order, I petition for exemption. I myself received a good exemption. The petition must be submitted by the end of this month [whether April or May unclear] to the Ministry of the Interior."[97]

He then asked his brother (in Budapest) if he could submit the petition documents, or if he (Samu) should send them directly to the Ministry. "I am glad that you and yours, modestly not drawing attention to yourselves, are able to stay together. May God grant that till the redemption you can stay like this."[98] Although Samu was to some extent observant, it is unlikely that by 'redemption' here he meant the messianic version envisioned by the Jewish religion. It is more likely that he simply meant liberation from the terrible processes of war, persecution, and occupation.

In another undated letter at about the same time- the very end of April or early May 1944 – Samu describes the days in which the ghettoization process took place:

"At seven in the morning a joint German-Hungarian committee visited me. I was still in bed. After a brief police procedure I was escorted to Vajay Utca 19, where I found myself together with eighty-two others, all old acquaintances and friends. But on Saturday of

---

[97] Undated letter, presumably written at the end of April or beginning of May, 1944.

[98] Ibid.

that same week I and fourteen others were sent home with the admonition to continue my medical practice. Psychologically-speaking it
was not any worse on the inside than it is on the outside; physically
we had good treatment, slept on straw, had good blankets. I myself
slept at least as well as at home. The Israelite congregation provided
us with food. Everyone [of the fifteen exempt] came home now, just
when the filling up of the "camp" [ghetto] has been going on for five
days. Only Laura and family are in there at Kolcsey-Batthany Street.
Tomorrow, our street [Arpad Utca] is next, but at least for now, we
are going to stay home. We, air-raid alarm managers, with wives and
children, can stay at home, and fortunately, because Zoli [Zoltan]
was called up and moved, he, too, can stay with us. Of course my
medical office had to be turned over; right now an engineering
office occupies it. Now my waiting room is in the hallway and the
medical office is upstairs, a dark room where we sometimes stay, or
in [another] room which was our bedroom lately. Zoli was called
up to serve in the management of airport construction; he serves as
an engineer there, somewhere in Transdanubia [western Hungary].
In this way he escaped the most horrific internment camp that ever
existed [referring to the Szatmár ghetto]. The worst lot is suffered by
the residents of Petöfi and Bathory Streets. Imagine, they each have
a bed area which is two meters long and one meter wide; twenty
to thirty people crammed into a room; so far, no word about food,
everyone eats from the bundle they carry; no one may enter the
room, or if they have entered, may not leave. We cannot offer any
kind of help. My medical practice, as you can imagine, given the
circumstances, almost equals zero."

My mother recounted the visit by the German-Hungarian committee in slightly different terms. She was struck by the great politeness of the German officers, to the point of being prepared to serve
them tea. She did not realize that this politeness was a common

tactic, used to keep the large Jewish population calm and in ignorance before the onslaught.[99]

Samu was able to help the inhabitants of the ghetto to some extent. The former chief physician and director of the Szatmár Jewish Hospital now set up a provisional hospital in a former straw-hat factory owned by David Grosz, at 37 Petöfy Street.[100] Other doctors joined him in this effort, along with some non-professional volunteers. They contrived to treat "ordinary" patients, the sick, the pregnant, the old, and those driven out of local hospitals and into the ghetto, irrespective of their condition. But they also tried to help the victims of torture who were left with crushed organs, broken limbs, and those suffering from sheer exposure to the elements and starvation. For not everyone in the ghetto was able to find space in an apartment; many slept in open yards and gardens on the bare ground.

Deportation to Auschwitz from Szatmár began on 19 May,1944, the larger process of deporting Transylvanian Jews having started in Maramarossighet (Elie Wiesel's hometown) on 16 May. Whatever was known about the final destination by that point by the Jewish Council in Budapest, that information was not conveyed to the Jews of the Hungarian provinces. They entered the trains without resistance.[101] There were six transports by train from Szatmár, each transport carrying about three thousand Jews, in appalling conditions which are well known. Physicians were scheduled for the

---

[99] Cf. Munkacsi, *How It Happened*, 23.

[100] Csirak and Elefant, *Szatmar Jews*, 41.

[101] I shall comment further on the topic of resistance below. Here we may simply note that non-resistance was also a central feature in the deportations of Polish Jews, as the historian Emanuel Ringelblum (in Warsaw) described at the time. The same is true of hundreds of thousands of Russian prisoners of war captured by the Germans. See Luis Raffeiner, *Wir waren keine Menschen mehr: Erinnerungen eines Wehrmacht Soldaten an die Ostfront*. Aufgezeichnet von Luise Ruatti, mit einem Nachwort von Hannes Heer (Bozen: Edition Raetia, 2010),68-69.

last transport from Szatmár on 1 June, but Samu did not wait. On 15 May he ended his own life. According to my mother, this took place upstairs in the medical office (by now the hallway) in his own home, by injection. His immediate family were permitted to exit the ghetto in the evening, under police guard, and attend the funeral in the Neolog cemetery. The service was conducted by Cantor Naftali Stern, who handled all thirty of the funerals that took place during this time. [102] At Rozsi's request, he was buried in a grave next to her father, Jakab Reiter, and not next to his own father, Albert Schwartz. Cantor Stern later reported that Rozsi did not believe that she herself would ever be buried near her family, where a plot had apparently already been purchased, and so she wanted Samu to be buried there.

My mother was deported with the transport of 26 May. An unofficial-looking, handwritten note, dated in 1946 – long after the deportations—states that In April 1944 she had converted to Christianity. The note is supposed to represent a conversion certificate retroactive to April 1944, and is signed by a pastor from the Reformed Church. [103] There had been tens of thousands of conversions in recent decades, for a variety of reasons, but the facticity of this supposed conversion strikes me as extremely doubtful. At this late date, April 1944, during the ghettoization process and when the irreversible nature of the deportations–even if only to some remote location for resettlement-- may have been at least suspected by my mother, it was more likely to have appeared pointless. Moreover, as mentioned above, my mother had long before (about 1942) made the choice to return to Szatmár from Budapest, where she might have remained in relative safety. It is much more likely that such a conversion certificate, whether legitimate or not (and it certainly does not look official in any way) was intended to serve some post-war purpose of survival.

Shortly before ghettoization and deportation, my mother's and

---

[102] Personal communication from Gyuri Elefant, June 2020.
[103] Cf. note 86 above.

Pál Janos' apartment in Budapest had been confiscated, in the extremely rapid and rough manner demanded by Eichmann. Starting on 4 April, all Budapest Jews had to vacate their homes within a day; leave behind all bedding and household items; turn over the keys to representatives from the Central Council of Hungarian Jews; and move into some specially designated buildings with a yellow star (which became part of the Budapest Ghetto).[104] The eviction/confiscation order received by my mother and her husband was signed by one Viola Freud. Since my mother was probably not in Budapest at any point in April, but still with her family in Szatmár and either in the ghetto or on the verge of being sent there, it is likely that Dezsö handled the expropriation process for her, presumably along with his own.

I don't know whether Zsuzsa and her little son Jani were on the same transport as my mother, or another one. Rozsi wrote a hasty note to Dezsö in Budapest; he or someone else marked it "received" on 2 June 1944, that is, one day after the last transport from Szatmár. In cryptic language Rozsi wrote: "My husband went to our parents [meaning the graveyard]. I myself and the children [i.e. Zsuzsa, Jani her son, and Kató] to Riza's [Samu's sister's place in the ghetto]. Please take into your hands our petition - please get in touch with Gyula Csenge, notary public. Tomorrow we are traveling."

Auschwitz and Zittau

The train journey to Auschwitz-Birkenau has often been described elsewhere, as has the nature of the camp itself. So I will not go into great detail about either one. Each train car was filled beyond capacity; there was barely room to stand, let alone sit or lie, for days on end. There was only one bucket for sanitation; no food, no water, no air. Many people died or fell into highly disturbed mental states

---

[104] Munkacsi, *How It Happened*, 54.

and illnesses. Upon arrival at Birkenau, those who were able to step
off the train, as opposed to falling out of it, dead, or being thrown
off it, were swiftly moved along the platform or ramp and separated
according to various factors determined by the SS: age and fitness for
work (go to the right); women with babies and small children (go to
the left, that is, to the gas chambers); the elderly and infirm of either
gender (to the left). My mother was thirty years old at this moment,
and quite healthy. She was directed to a barracks housing Hungarian
Jewish women and from there to heavy labor of some kind. It is not
clear to me where exactly she worked while at Auschwitz; she mentioned airplane parts, but may have foreshortened the story, because
that was the type of work she did at another camp later. Be that as it
may, she was at Birkenau from May till October 1944. She endured
the notorious early- morning roll calls (*Appell*), when the starving,
dehydrated, overworked and exhausted, often extremely sick prisoners had to stand for hours, or collapsed on the spot; the overcrowded,
lice-infested bunk beds, with people sleeping on top of one another;
the starvation rations; the lack of sanitation; and so on. A document
located by the International Tracing Service records that a certain
Zsuzsa Borosc, that is, a woman with exactly the same name as
my mother's sister, was imprisoned in Auschwitz-Birkenau on 3
November 1944. If this was indeed the sister, it would mean that
immediately after deportation and arrival from Szatmár at the end of
May, with her small son, she was not gassed, but was "occupied" in
some other way at another part of the camp. Upon being transferred
to Birkenau, this Zsuzsa was placed in the Hygiene Institute of the
Waffen-SS, where a variety of "medical" and extremely inhumane
experiments on human beings were conducted.

By the fall of 1944, the Allies were increasing their bombing of
nearby Auschwitz-Monowitz, which produced rubber, chemicals and
other much-needed products. They had also gained air supremacy
over large parts of Eastern Europe, Hungary and Austria, thereby
endangering the Germans' production of aircraft and weaponry.

The Nazis –that is, Hitler and Speer-- decided to move aircraft- and weapons- production underground, within Austria and the Reich itself. Consequently, thousands of slave-laborers, mainly Jewish, were moved from Auschwitz to other camps, in particular Mauthausen and Mittelbau-Dora. I presume that it was as part of this general process that my mother was moved from Auschwitz-Birkenau to *Konzentrationslager* Zittau, in October 1944.

The huge Junker manufacturing company—*Junker Flugzeug und Motorenwerke* -- obtained permission in September 1944 to transfer part of its production processes to the town of Zittau in Lower Silesia, in the area known in German as the *Dreiländereck,* between Germany, Poland and Czechoslovakia.[105] Junker was to take over a factory building belonging to a textile company in Zittau (Herwigsdorferstrasse 4b); textile production remained the "cover story" for what the Nazis called the "Zittwerke." The workers/slave labor for this aircraft- parts production was provided by Hungarian, Polish and Slovakian Jewish women imported from Auschwitz. After my mother's contingent, one or two more arrived, for a total of about 800 women. Among the 450 women brought in in October was my mother. The women were housed in a former prisoner-of-war camp for Russian prisoners in World War I, in a small town not far from Zittau called Grossporitsch. This small camp at Grossporitsch was considered an external camp (*Aussenlager*) or sub-camp of the larger Gross-Rosen camp, which contained about 125,000 prisoners. There were many other sub-camps for Gross-Rosen. In Zittau the laborers worked on motors for Junker's Jumo 004B aircraft. The products were shipped by train to assembly plants (*Montageorten*) in Bavaria.

Supervision of the laborers at Grossporitsch and Zittau was shared by an air force (*Luftwaffe*) unit housed in the Beckmann

---

[105] Sächsische Landeszentrale fur politische Bildung/Umweltbibliothek Grosshennersdorf e.V. (Hrsg), *Erinnerungs-und Gedenkorte im sächischen Dreiländereck Polen-Tschechien-Deutschland* (Dresden: Sächsische Landeszentrale für politische Bildung, 2020).

Department Store; two infantry units which were also nearby; and the 17. SS-Totenkopf Wachbataillon, one of the most fearsome SS units in existence. A Soviet air attack on 7 May 1945 allowed most of the prisoners, including my mother, to escape the camp as well as to get away from the oncoming Soviet Army, which had an extremely poor record in regard to conquered territory: rape and looting were carried out on an enormous scale. While some of the prisoners died of exhaustion and disease before they could even get to the outskirts of the small town of Zittau, my mother was able to do so. She then made her way, over many weeks, on foot and in part by train, back to Szatmár.

Afterwards

Budapest-Sydney-Montreal

I don't know why, but after working for the International Committee of the Red Cross (with the permission of the U.S. Military Government) for a several months, my father sought and found work in Budapest rather than his hometown of Vienna. As Vienna, like Budapest, was in the Soviet zone of occupation, there was at that moment -late summer 1945-- little or no difference from the point of view of state sovereignty and citizenship: both countries had to negotiate terms for their provisional governments with the Allies, but with the Soviets on their territory. But it had been seven years since my father had left Vienna under very exigent circumstances; he no doubt first wanted to see if he could find any of his family in Szatmár. Failing that, he decided to look for work in Budapest, where he may also have hoped to meet again people he had known between 1938-1942. An International Tracing Service document shows him returning to Szatmár on 10 August 1945. By his own account, he was then placed under medical supervision in Budapest, in the care of Drs. Slezak and Adler. I don't recall whether this treatment was physical or psychological, but I do recall my father saying that he was profoundly depressed for several months at that point.

Nonetheless, a personal identification card dated 29 August 1945 shows him living at Phönix Utca 7 in the V. District of Budapest. A trade union membership card (Free Trade Union of Hungarian

Engineers and Technicians), issued on 29 August 1946, lists him as having been a member and employed at the Obuda shipyards since 16 October 1945, and residing at Rona Utca 165 in the XIV. District. A document issued in turn by the Obuda shipyard, "property of the Russian State," on 3 January 1947, shows that he had been chief engineer and shop manager but was temporarily transferred to the drafting department due to a shortage in personnel. Another document, from October 1947, shows that he was indeed transferred back to the position of chief mechanical engineer, assigned to a project for the construction of a thirty-five ton floating crane for the Transportation Ministry.

The crane project was related to reconstruction of Budapest's renowned bridges, especially the Chain Bridge, which my father mentioned as having fallen within his responsibilities. The bridges had been destroyed on 18 January 1945 by the Germans. Between December 1944 and February 1945, the city was under siege by Soviet and Romanian forces, and destruction of the bridges was part of an effort to create re-supply problems for the Allies. The Obuda Shipyard, where the engineers worked, was located, as was its later competitor the Ganz-Danubius factory (which had once served the Austro-Hungarian Imperial Navy), on an island in the Danube. It had been built by Count István Szechenyi in 1835, in collaboration with the Austrian company *Erste Donaudampfschiffahrtsgesellschaft* (First Danube Steamship Travel Company). Count Széchenyi (1791-1860) who grew up in both Vienna and Nagyczenk (site of my father's later internment), also sponsored the original construction of the Chain Bridge, one of the greatest bridges in the world at the time (1849), and a symbol of communication between West and East. Széchenyi was a prominent and nationally known figure throughout his lifetime, the family having historical relations with the Hapsburg, Esterhazy and Liechtenstein families. His own father founded the Hungarian National Library. István Széchenyi promoted all kinds of economic development in Central and Eastern

Europe, as well as international projects relating to what we would today call integrated water resource management.

By 1947, my father and mother had met again, having probably last seen each other in late 1941 or early 1942, before my father and all other Hungarian Jewish men were forced into labor battalions. My mother had traveled, at some point after her liberation in May 1945, from Szatmár to Budapest. Perhaps she wanted to see what had become of her former possessions there, or to find her uncle Dezsö and his family. Her husband Pál Janos Adonyi had not returned from labor service; his death was recorded on a military list as having taken place on 11 March 1943 in Ukraine. This may have occurred in connection with the Hungarian Army's retreat from the Voronezh, or in some other way during the aftermath of the Battle of Stalingrad, but it could also have been at any other location where labor servicemen had been deployed. In any case my mother had also heard, through a friend who had run into him by chance, that my father was living and working in Budapest. She decided to look him up. They were married on 19 April 1947, and lived at Erzsébet Place 13, Apt.3, in the VII District, probably in the same apartment building in which she had lived with Pál Janos Adonyi.

Despite finding some contentment through his engineering work, my father was increasingly unhappy about the political situation. As I recall, he told me (many years later) that he simply could not tolerate living under yet another tyrannical system. Indeed the transition from the authoritarian Horthy regime to Soviet control of Hungary (and other parts of Eastern Europe)was well underway.

As early as fall 1944, a Provisional Government in Hungary had been set up under the supervision of, and as it were in the wake of, the Red Army. At that point, the Soviet strategy involved deferring a move to fully communist rule in Hungary.[106] Stalin was concentrating on the strategically more- important Sovietization of Poland and East Germany, and did not want to expend resources or political capital in relations with the West in order to "force the end" in less -important Hungary. The result was a coalition or national front-type of Provisional Government, in which not only local communists were represented but also émigré communists who had spent much of the war in Moscow, as well as representatives from the previous Horthy government.[107] While this relatively loose hold by the Soviets on Hungarian politics could not entirely distract from facts on the ground, it did buy time. For the facts on the ground were extremely ugly: individual soldiers of the Red Army engaged in widespread theft, extortion, murder and above all rape, including frequent gang rape. In the countryside and smaller towns, communists were able to set up 1919-style soviets or councils, carry out land "reform," and use red- terror tactics. In the name of reparations, the Soviets dismantled large sections of Hungarian economic infrastructure, such as factories and all their fittings, and transported them back to the Soviet Union. Hungary was also required to provision the Red Army, despite the general degradation of agriculture, widespread food and fuel shortages in the urban centers, and lack of means of transportation of goods.

Gradually, however, between 1944 and 1949, and especially after 1947, with the Soviet-Yugoslav split, Soviet policy in Hungary changed and became more focused on complete communist domination and control. After 1947, ideological and practical conformity to Stalin's views and aims became essential. Opposition parties were aggressively eliminated. While in principle free parliamentary

---

[106] The following account is based on: Martin Mevius, *Agents of Moscow:The Hungarian Communist Party and the Origins of Socialist Patriotism 1941-1953* (Oxford: Clarendon Press,2005); Anne Applebaum, *Iron Curtain: The Crushing of Eastern Europe 1944-1956* (New York: Anchor Books, 2013).
[107] Mevius, *Agents,* 53.

elections could take place, in practice the Communist Party, backed by the Soviets, used violence, vote fraud, and propaganda to undermine other parties and to ensure its own victories. The atmosphere became increasingly oppressive and undemocratic. In the public sphere as well, Soviet symbols replaced historical or traditional ones; Erzsebet Square, where my parents lived, was renamed Stalin Square in 1946.[108] All decisions, down to the texts of political programs and announcements, resided ultimately not only with party offices in Moscow, but with Stalin.

Nor had antisemitism disappeared. As in Poland and elsewhere in Europe, it lived on, despite the catastrophe which had taken place. Although (or because) several of the communist party leaders in Hungary were of Jewish origin - Mátyás Rákosi, Ernö Gerö, Mihály Farkas, and Jozsef Revai–resentment toward returning forced laborers like my father, and other Jews, was considerable. There was fear of their influence in the Communist party itself (though most returning laborers, like my father, were far from becoming members of the party), fear that they might be able to reverse the land "reform," fear that they would somehow undermine negotiations on population resettlements with Czechoslovakia and Romania. Hostility was rampant and fantastical, and the Hungarian Communists began to turn on each other as well as on the Jews. Thus, while in 1945 and 1946 war crimes and treason trials of former Arrow Cross and Horthy government leaders were held, by 1949 the Interior Minister himself, Laszlo Rajk, a Communist from early on, was on trial on trumped -up charges of intrigue with Western powers against the Soviet Union, national deviationism, and Trotsykite and Titoist deviationism. The indictment was copy-edited, so to speak, by Stalin himself. Rákosi wrote to Georgi Dimitrov, leader of the Communist International and Prime Minister of Bulgaria, regarding the ruthless tactics needed to rid the Communist Party of Jews, to suppress the

[108] Ibid., 205.

role of Jews in the country altogether, and of the reputation of the Hungarian Communist Party of being both too Jewish and antisemitic: "I am afraid there is some truth in both."[109]

My father's concerns about remaining in Hungary were, therefore, exceedingly well-founded. In April 1949 he and my mother boarded a train for Vienna with one suitcase each, and sought escape from the European continent, having exhausted all possibilities for remaining at home there. From Vienna they were transferred, through the emigration service of the American Joint Distribution Committee (based in Paris) to Genoa in July. After a not-unpleasant stay in Genoa, they boarded the ship "Napoli," which took them to Australia and old Szatmár friends, Anuska and László Vidor. The Vidors had left Szatmár long before the war, and were able to serve as sponsors.

From 1949 to 1953 my father worked at the Dunlop Rubber Company in Sydney. In 1953 he began a gradual shift to academic life, becoming a university lecturer in mechanical engineering at the University of New South Wales, and then in 1957 at the University of Sydney. Between 1953 and 1961, in addition to lecturing, he wrote an introductory textbook, *Strength of Materials for Engineers* (London: Pitman & Sons Publishers, 1959) in the area of materials science, and obtained a Master of Science degree from the University of Sydney in 1961. He was able to arrange a sabbatical year in 1963, during which he completed a doctorate at the University of Vienna, and subsequent research at the Technische Hochschule Aachen.

It was during this first decade in Sydney that I was born. My parents were at that point living in Rose Bay, and I have an early memory of playing under the table in a Greek café nearby that they frequented. From there we moved to the comfortable northern suburb of East Gordon, across the Sydney Harbor Bridge. I recall all kinds of fruit trees (peach, banana) at the back of an enormous

---

[109] Ibid., 97.

garden, which my father enjoyed tending, as well as a long row of rose bushes that he planted along a walkway in the front. On weekends there were excursions to Whale Beach, where in- between swims we ate fish and chips. I enjoyed watching the lifeguards, zinc cream lathered on their noses, practicing their rescue techniques. When we weren't at the beach we visited the Vidor family in their large house in Dover Heights; in my mind's eye I see the angles of a glaringly white, multi-story house reaching to the cerulean sky near the water, a fit subject for a David Hockney painting. No doubt it was a pleasure for my parents to be property owners, and substantial citizens, once again. But while a Central or Eastern European immigrant Jew could be a citizen, he could not be an Australian. Eventually, underlying cultural differences between European and Australian academics, and perhaps a hint of old-fashioned social antisemitism, would drive my father to seek a position in the broader melting pot of North America.

It is perhaps at this point, when my father was in his early fifties, that the only genuinely happy phase of his life began, fulfilled through academic achievement, secure living conditions, and international travel and friendships. During the sabbatical year, my father was offered positions at the University of Illinois-Champaign, the University of Toronto, and McGill University. Acquiescing in my mother's strong desire to live in an environment with a more European flavor, he accepted the position at McGill in Montreal. After a quick return trip to Sydney to sell the house and to settle all the other matters involved in a trans-Pacific move, and another voyage back to Vancouver on a P&O ocean liner, we moved into an apartment on Kensington Avenue, in the leafy, again very English, neighborhood of Westmount in Montreal. The view from the living room window was of Westmount's emerald-colored bowling green, with the slim and fit bowling club members dressed in starchy white skirts and slacks. The apartment building was also literally next door to *Shaar Hashomayim*, one of Canada's largest and most prestigious

Traditional synagogues. My parents were assiduous in not setting foot in there; they had had enough of Jewish life and death. On my wedding day some fifteen years later, they did enter it, but reluctantly and slightly amazed that there would be no adverse consequences.

My father served as Professor of Mechanical Engineering at McGill from 1966 to 1980, with a named professorship -Thomas Workman Professor-- being awarded in 1970. He taught classes in continuum mechanics; the theory of elasticity; statistical thermo-dynamics; and other fields. He established a research laboratory, the Micromechanics of Solids Laboratory, which used laser tech-nology and electron microscopy to study the deformation of ma-terials under intense heat. He published more than ninety research papers, and two monographs relating to the micromechanics of solids. He delivered numerous invited lectures, for example at the Polish Academy of Sciences (Warsaw, 1975, 1976); The Seventh International Congress of Rheology (Goteborg, Sweden, 1976); and the Fourteenth International Congress of Theoretical and Applied Mechanics (Delft University, The Netherlands, 1976), in addition he gave many somewhat less formal talks and lectures, from the California Institute of Technology to the University of Kyoto, Japan. He received research grants from the National Research Council of Canada, Atomic Energy of Canada at Chalk River, Ontario, the Pulp and Paper Research Institute and the U.S. Army Research center in Durham, NC, and spent a remarkable year as a fellow at the *Wissenschaftskolleg* in Berlin. As the stay in Berlin and repeated visits to Poland indicate, whatever memories of the antisemitic past had stayed with him, he was not going to let this stand in the way of his life in international science. At a particularly memorable conference in 1976 in Kielce, Poland (site of a major postwar po-grom) organized by the distinguished academician Henryk Zorski, my father felt comfortable enough to reveal some of his musical abilities, buried since his youth in Vienna: with another scientist on drums, he launched into a virtuoso jazz piano performance. It was an evening of extraordinary collegiality among scientists of both West and East, in a communist "rest home" in the still antisemitic Polish countryside.

Technically my father retired in 1977, but remained emeritus professor and an active researcher until 1995, when he suffered a major heart attack. He died four years later, after a stroke, at the Jewish General Hospital on Côte des Neiges.

My mother, meanwhile, loved her friends in the group called the Womens' Associates of McGill, with whom she played bridge and attended lectures at the McGill University Faculty Club. But she also reveled in the Francophone culture of the city. She became a substitute French teacher at Westmount High School around the corner, and frequently attended French-language plays at the Théâtre du Rideau Vert. It became a significant Sunday winter afternoon ritual (before climate change, when the snow was often more than knee-deep) for the two of us to go to one of the French-language cinemas on Park Avenue in the city's east end, and to have a warm and aromatic cappuccino afterwards in order to discuss the latest film. Indeed, the aromas of the city loom large in my own memories of Montreal: the smoke from my father's endless cigarettes as we walked down snowy Stanley Street, downtown, for yet another coffee in a Hungarian-owned coffee shop; the bakeries everywhere, on St. Laurent Avenue, on Greene Avenue, and the Patisserie Gascogne on Sherbrooke Street, where one could hardly sit down between the excited shoppers. I can't help but suspect that unspoken, all along, was a sad, unfulfillable desire on all our parts to recapture something of what had been lost in Vienna, Budapest and Szatmár.

My mother had a few Hungarian Jewish lady friends, one who had had similar wartime experiences, and several who had escaped in better circumstances. Apart from her cousin, Livia Reiter, who landed up in Toronto, there was Klara Rosenfeld, who was not from Szatmár but another town. She had been at Auschwitz and later lived with her husband in Tangiers, before settling in Montreal. The other was Sári Verin, née Gerö, from Szatmár. Sári was three years younger than my mother, but the girls had attended the same convent school in Szatmár, gone ice-skating on the nearby Samos River, and had known each other's parents. Sári's father, Sandor Gerö, a wealthy businessman, was severely tortured in the Szatmár ghetto and subsequently committed suicide.

The three ladies - Kató, Klari and Sári-- often met for lunch on Saturdays with a small group of other Hungarian Jewish women, in Westmount Square. While it was not quite the renowned Café Gerbeaud in Budapest, or the Café Central in Vienna, it was an elegant venue, with expensive clothing boutiques, highly polished brass fixtures and camel-colored leather chairs, a variety of imported and fine foods, and Westmount's wealthiest, best-dressed citizens going about their innocent weekend activities. I often thought, as the hours for my own academic work slipped away, that there must be some meaning to these little gatherings. But to my unspoken disappointment, the intense discussions and analyses of past and present never arrived at anything I could call an explanation. As Philip Roth said somewhere, the meaning of life is [just] that it stops. On the other hand, these ladies displayed a level of life-affirmation, family warmth and elegance which was extremely valiant and, I think, quite inimitable.

After my father's death in August,1999, my mother and I continued to try to live as we had done, given that I did not live in Montreal any longer. Summer stays in the Laurentians, or in Maine, or Prince Edward Island. The French cinemas on Park Avenue. But the city changed gradually, and my mother, of course, grew older and much more tired. She died of congestive heart failure in the Royal Victoria Hospital on *erev yom kippur*, 2010.

Conclusion

As the epigraph to this book is intended to show, in preparing to write about my parents I have been struck by the enormity of the difference between writing in an impersonal and general way for an academic audience in the way that I usually do, and writing about the most personal, family matters. While on the one hand I would like to be able to conclude, from my parents' lives, something about history, religion, and totalitarian politics, I also feel that this would be presumptuous in a text about lives other than my own, lives which endured historically unprecedented events. They themselves never offered any analyses. Perhaps they needed all their remaining energies for their new lives, or perhaps they simply continued what Hermann Broch had called the pre-World War I, Central European "flight into the apolitical."[110] I can only discover whatever conclusions they may have reached through the little they said and through their conduct. I have therefore placed my own few, larger-scale reflections, which touch on religion and politics, in a separate section below.

I can say that while my parents demonstrated extraordinary resilience, and no-one would have guessed their histories from their comportment, the Shoah remained a deep undercurrent. While rarely spoken of, it guided the three of us silently, in different ways. My mother was quite determined to see it in an episodic way: it was an utterly catastrophic but nonetheless relatively short period of history and of her own life, and it was best to try to turn to a new type of normalcy. In practice this meant living in warm friendship with intelligent, goal-directed people; staying as healthy as possible; being in contact with nature and natural beauty as much as possible; not making a fuss about small inconveniences. It also meant taking

---

[110] Hermann Broch, *Hugo von Hoffmannsthal and His Time: The European Imagination 1860-1920*. Translated and with an Introduction by Michael P. Steinberg (Chicago: University of Chicago Press, 1984).

a generous, cosmopolitan view of the world, though with a cosmo-politanism firmly rooted in Central and Western Europe; being by- and -large socially and culturally tolerant, even while retaining a fair amount of Hapsburg formality; and yet not falling under any illusions about widespread dishonesty, greed and corruption. My mother's favorite term for the latter was 'perfidiousness.' On the other hand, at certain moments, especially at holiday times, a deep grief rose to the surface and my mother missed her pre-war family intensely, without shedding a tear.

My father shared much of this outlook, but I believe was af-fected by a long-term and deep-seated depression which was only disguised by the energy he brought to his academic research and his apparent enjoyment of simple pleasures, such as drinking coffee and smoking. While a firm believer in the utility --in J.S. Mill's sense of contributing to the wellbeing of humanity-- of scientific progress, he occasionally wondered aloud about the meaning of life, and was be-wildered and disturbed by the amount of time that had been lost in his own life through circumstances utterly beyond his control. This is what Imre Kertesz expressed in the closing pages of *Fateless*ness:

"After all, there are times when twenty minutes, in and of them-selves, can be quite a lot of time…[When] it comes down to it, each and every minute something else might have happened other than what actually did happen, at Auschwitz just as much as, let's suppose, here at home…"[111]

It sometimes made my father highly impatient, even angry, at what he saw as unnecessary obstacles in everyday life, such as waiting in a dentist's office. But he never expressed a word of anger toward those who had actually been responsible for what happened to him, or toward Germany and Hungary in a national sense. Perhaps he thought it was a waste of time and energy, especially now that he had achieved a measure of security and success in a more rational,

---

[111] Imre Kertesz, *Fatelessness. A Novel.* Translated from the Hungarian by Tim Wilkinson (New York: Vintage International, 2004), 258.

prosperous, and liberal part of the world. Or perhaps he felt, understandably, that no merely human indictment could ever be adequate to the crimes that had been committed.

It must be said, however, that although my parents did not give explicit expression to particular political views or principles, they repeatedly demonstrated a form of humanitarianism. My father liked to share a cigarette and quiet chat with a workman, and felt deeply though unostentatiously with the sick or bereaved. My mother followed humanitarian crises around the world, and made a point of distributing food that might otherwise be wasted to the homeless. These attitudes, and my parents' appreciation of nature, influenced my own later interests in both international human rights and problems of water security, and as a university administrator I attempted to further these causes to the extent possible.

The downside of my parents' views, for me, was that, given what had actually happened to them, very few contemporary problems of my own could be considered serious. This, in turn, meant that I had little sense of right or entitlement. This was a significant lack, not only on a personal level but on a political one as well. However, the main effect on me, as already indicated in the Preface, was a profound, twofold desire: to understand what had happened and how it happened; and to find an answer to the further question (modifying the title of a short essay by Emmanuel Levinas) as to how Judaism is still possible. While a thorough-going philosophical response to this particular question would be out of place here, I would like to offer some preliminary, general reflections.

II Essay: Does the Holocaust Have Any Meaning? Jewish Thought After the Holocaust

Introduction

I have found no better way to articulate my general stance toward the Shoah than the words of the Israeli philosopher Shalom Rosenberg:

"Just as standing upon sacred ground requires us to remove our shoes...so do I feel myself obligated, when writing about the Holocaust, so to speak to remove my academic robe—and to declare that I am not speaking in the name of any academic discipline, but purely in terms of my own most intimate feelings...From a religious viewpoint, I wish to say that the memory of the Holocaust is also holy in my eyes! The testimonies and experiences of the survivors... are holy."[112]

This should not be taken to mean, however, that I agree that there is any religious meaning to the Shoah; as I will discuss further below, I don't think there is any such meaning. While there are political and perhaps moral lessons to be drawn from it, I don't believe

---

[112] Shalom Rosenberg, "The Holocaust: Lessons, Explanations, Meanings," in: Steven Katz (ed.), *Wrestling with God: Jewish Theological Responses during and after the Holocaust* (Oxford: Oxford University Press, 2007), 333.

that it represented the fulfilment of any divine intention or purpose, certainly not one that could be comprehended by human beings. But I do wish to convey that it is a set of events and phenomena which should be treated with the utmost respect, sensitivity, and even reverence. Nor would I go so far as Rosenberg and add the claim that "the studies of the experts, the theories of the thinkers, and the lessons learned by the politicians are the most profane of the profane... ."[113] On the contrary, I believe that there are important and fairly specific political implications arising from the enormous work done by historians, legal scholars, and political scientists, regardless of whatever stances may be taken by everyday politicians. There are, in addition, some illuminating scientific studies available in social and political psychology; these relate to crowd behavior and willingness to inflict punishment (the famous Milgram experiment). I am conscious, rather, of the extreme frailty of theology and philosophy in this context.

It is neither possible nor necessary to restate here the explanations provided by historical researchers over the past seventy years as to who Hitler and the Nazis were, how they came to power, and how they functioned while in power. The works of British, American, and German scholars, as well as many others in Eastern Europe, run into the thousands and have made both the general outlines as well as many details quite clear. What once seemed a totally incomprehensible set of events, a *mysterium tremendum*, has become to a large extent intelligible on the political, military and social-psychological levels. While there continue to be detailed debates about intentionality versus functionality in the causation of the Holocaust, ideological versus material causes for the war, biographical versus social- structural approaches, and many other issues, we know enough now to see more than approximately how it all came about. Indeed we are now better able to recognize authoritarian and

---

[113] Ibid.

genocidal trends when we see them. In my estimation, what remains quite unexplained, if not inexplicable, is the human capacity for extreme cruelty and, to use a not very enlightening word, evil. To understand actions such as throwing babies into a burning furnace, shoving wheelchair-bound, sick old men out of apartment-building windows, shooting terrified parents and children into ditches, this is incomprehensible to any sentient being with natural compassion. All we have by way of explanation here is that the brutalizing effects of World War I, and decades of civic violence in Central and Eastern Europe (including the Russian Revolution of 1917), must have been far greater than has been fully appreciated. Either that, or we have to resort to some sort of innate capacity for cruelty. In any case, this was not merely what philosophers and theologians have called the privation or absence of goodness; it was a phenomenon of active cruelty and violence on a scale beyond comparison.

I turn now first to some political reflections, and then to the religious.

The Holocaust in Hungary

Within a decade after the end of World War II, while the survivors, both Jewish and non-Jewish, were still trying to build up new lives in a largely shattered world, recriminations, largely but not only from Israel, started to flow. Given the experience of the neighboring Slovakian Jews earlier, in 1942, so the criticisms went, could the Hungarian Jews not have anticipated what would happen to them and leave or organize an effective resistance? Why did the leaders of Hungarian Jewry, based in Budapest, as well as the local Jewish Councils, behave in such apparently accommodating ways toward the Germans? These well- known and, to my mind, abhorrent criticisms from people who were not "there," have been refuted in various ways. The basic answer should be obvious to anyone who has studied the situation: mass exodus and effective resistance were simply not possible. As early as 1938, when the First Jewish Law was passed in Hungary, many Jews were deprived of the financial wherewithal to depart, even if they could obtain transit papers of some kind, a very difficult process. And at that point those who, like my grandparents, still had homes and owned property, were hoping to be able, through lawsuits and connections, to be able to hold on to it. There was also the hope, all along, that the Hungarian government, which seemed to be able to keep Hitler at arm's length, and had historically protected Jews to some extent, would be able to continue to do so. The Hungarian Jews could not "get their minds around" the thought that Germany would actually invade and that the Hungarian government would be forced to yield. This theme recurs frequently in Hungarian memoirs, and not only by Jews. It was certainly a point of view widely shared in Szatmár and which was later emphatically expressed to me by my mother. Elie Wiesel, as it were down the road in Sighet, stated it thus:

"The truth is that, in spite of everything we knew about Nazi Germany, we had an inexplicable confidence in German culture and humanism…We all fell into the trap history had set for us. During World War I the German army had rescued Jews who, under Russian occupation, had been beaten, ridiculed and oppressed by savage Cossacks whose mentality and traditions were steeped in anti-Semitism. … The German officers had been courteous and helpful … Lulled by memories of the Germans of that era, the Jews refused to believe that their sons could be inhuman. In this the Jews were not alone."[114]

Moreover, the true nature and extent of the exterminations which had already taken place were *not* fully understood or *rec*ognized, either by Jews or non-Jews, in the provinces of Hungary as late as March 1944. The written report by Slovakian escapees

---

[114] Wiesel, *All Rivers,*27.

from Auschwitz –with precise descriptions of the structure and function of the camp-- was not complete until 27 April. By that time the ghettoization process in Hungary had begun and one train transport had already left.[115] Further, there is considerable evidence that both Western authorities and Western Jews made efforts, for various reasons, to suppress information about the extermination process as early as 1942. News reached the Polish National Council in London, and the World Jewish Congress in New York, in late 1942. Important figures such as Felix Frankfurter, Isaiah Berlin, Nahum Goldman and David Ben-Gurion could not bring themselves to believe that a plan for total annihilation was underway; they could perceive "only" a massive pogrom.[116] Be that as it may, Wiesel's memoir turns the tables on later (including Jewish) critics of Hungarian-Jewish weakness:

"It was April 1944, just a few weeks before the Allied landing in Normandy, but the Jews of Sighet had not been informed of the ramifications of the Final Solution. The free world, including Jewish leaders in America and Palestine, had known since 1942, but we knew nothing. Why didn't they warn us? Free Jews did not do all they could to save the Jews of Europe."[117]

Wiesel's argument here is that, although rescue operations on the ground would have been impossible–just as it was impossible for Jews to leave-- because of the ubiquitous and tight hold of the German military on European territory, it would have been possible

---

[115] Fenyö, *Hitler-Horthy*, 187. Rudolf Vrba, "The Preparations for the Holocaust in Hungary: An Eyewitness Account," in Randolph L. Braham and Scott Miller (eds.), *The Nazis' Last Victims: The Holocaust in Hungary* (Detroit: Wayne State University Press, 2002), 81.

[116] Braham, *Politics*, Vol.1 [?], 34; David Wyman, *The Abandonment of the Jews: America and the Holocaust 1941-1945* (New York: Pantheon Books,1984); Walter Laqueur, *The Terrible Secret: Suppression of the Truth about Hitler's 'Final Solution'* (Harmondsworth: Penguin Books Ltd., 1982).

[117] Wiesel, *All Rivers*, 63.

to give warnings by radio, to which Hungarian Jews did have access. They could have, says Wiesel, urgently proclaimed: "Don't let yourselves be locked in ghettoes, don't get into cattle cars!". While in Budapest various forms of rescue were achieved by diplomats in the Japanese and Portugese consulates, and by the Swedish Raoul Wallenberg, the hundreds of thousands of Jews in the provinces were "sacrificed, abandoned and betrayed."[118] I, for one, tend to doubt whether a refusal to enter the ghettoes or to board the trains would have been successful to any great extent without significant coordination, and perhaps not even then. Although it is true that German military and police manpower was stretched to the limit, they still had substantial and willing Hungarian police forces to lean on to enforce the deportations.

Resistance, it seems to me, would mainly end in death, not liberation. The total control over the death and concentration camps, and, again, the domination of much of European territory by the German military and police forces, made escape and/or armed resistance almost completely impossible. While within the ghettos and camps there were some attempts at organized, armed resistance (the most famous being the Warsaw Ghetto Uprising in 1943, with others taking place in Auschwitz and the Bialystok Ghetto, for example), these were quite quickly, thoroughly and brutally crushed. And who has the retrospective right to gainsay a remaining desire and hope to go on living, after all? As Imre Kertész was to write a few years later about his time at Buchenwald:

"[F]rom far off I recognized...a whiff of turnip soup in the acrid air. A pity, because it must have been that spectacle, that aroma, which cut through my numbness to trigger an emotion, the growing waves of which were able to squeeze, even from my dried-out eyes, a few warmer drops amid the dankness that was soaking my face. Despite all deliberation, sense, insight, and sober reason, I could not

---

[118] Ibid., 64.

fail to recognize within myself the furtive and yet—ashamed as it might be, so to say of its irrationality—increasingly insistent voice of some muffled craving of sorts: I would like to live a little bit longer in this beautiful concentration camp."[119]

Perhaps more important with regard to the Holocaust in Hungary than the question of resistance is again the question, already discussed above: why did Germany invade Hungary at such a late stage in the war, and why were the Hungarian Gendarmerie and many civilians so eager to help carry out Hitler's (via Eichmann and Veesenmeyer) genocidal plans? Why did the Hungarians provide the extensive and intensive contributions in the form of anti-Jewish legislation, troops and the labor service system? These and related questions have become the subject of considerable debate among historians of Hungary. One authoritative response comes from Randolph L. Braham: "The decision to occupy Hungary resulted from a series of complex political/military factors: the unsolved 'Jewish question,' though important, was not the determining one."[120] Several historians have elaborated on this view by arguing that the Germans only decided on complete extermination of Hungarian Jewry once they had entered the country and found-- to their own surprise—very willing collaborators, not only in the highest offices of the land, but in lower echelons of the civil service and police forces.[121]

A comment from Hitler's plenipotentiary in Hungary, Veesenmeyer, during his trial in a Hungarian People's Court in 1946 supports this view:

"Had the Hungarians consistently refused to meet the German demands concerning the solution of the Jewish question, this solution would not have taken place. Pressure would certainly have been

---

[119] Kertesz, *Fatelessness*, 189.

[120] Braham, *Politics,* Vol.1,362.

[121] Gerlach und Aly, *Letzte Kapitel*, 250; Krisztián Ungváry, "Master Plan? The Decision-Making Process behind the Deportations," in Braham and Kovács (eds.), *Holocaust in Hungary*, 105-146.

applied, but as 1944 was already a year of 'crisis,' no force would have been available to collect and deport one million persons. ... Only the aid of the Hungarian Government made it possible to carry out the deportations so quickly and smoothly."[122]

While Veesenmayer's statement could be seen merely as an attempt to distribute the blame for the Holocaust in Hungary more equitably, it may well be true. In spring 1944, the war was not going in Germany's favor. The Germans were losing ground steadily in Poland and Ukraine as well as in the West, where there had been alternative agricultural resources; supplies for military and for defensive fortifications were becoming much scarcer. It is doubtful whether Hitler could have or would have expended the necessary resources to carry out the extermination without large-scale Hungarian aid. The use of local forces, moreover, had worked well in other parts of Eastern Europe. For example, in Estonia only 139 German officials were needed for the occupation; 800 Estonians constituted the security police.[123] In each case, and in Hungary, the local population was motivated to a large extent by the prospect of immediate material gain, as well by traditional forms of religious antisemitism. Throughout the Eastern European lands

"[p]olicemen robbed Jews or were rewarded for participation in the murder by sharing among themselves the possessions of the victims. Many policemen were semi-literate; peasants became the predominant element in the police forces...The sense of authority and power, especially for those who had previously occupied low rungs of the social hierarchy, combined with material benefits, were too attractive to resist."[124]

On the other hand, to say, as Veesenmeyer did, that in case of Hungarian hesitation "pressure would have been applied," was a huge understatement. It conceals, among other things, the intense

---

[122] Quoted in Levai, *Black Book*, 114.
[123] Prusin, *The Lands Between*, 164
[124] Ibid., 171.

ideological commitment and determination of Adolf Eichmann. Although he was ordered to go to work in Hungary, he believed wholly in the "value" of the extermination program. Bettina Stangneth has shown to what extent Eichmann's evil was *not* banal; he was crafty, intelligent, and completely depraved. He knew exactly how to apply the required murderous techniques in Hungary, as he had done elsewhere. If he had not relentlessly driven the Hungarians forward, I venture to say that, whatever other kinds of persecution they may have perpetrated, the Hungarian colleagues probably would not have undertaken large-scale ghettoization and deportation on their own initiative.[125]

We also saw that as early as 1938 Göring was intensely pre-occupied with securing the natural material resources for conduct of the war and had helped secure the *Anschluss* of Austria to that end. By the spring of 1944, both Hungary and Romania, with their important resources, were known to be seeking to change sides in the war. Oil, bauxite and other resources were needed more urgently than ever for continuing the war effort. Hitler had made it clear at least a year beforehand that an actual, physical intervention was likely, especially in light of Hungary's apparent unwillingness to go further in regard to "the Jewish question." A report from a 17 April 1943 meeting between Hitler, Horthy, von Ribbentrop and Döme Sztójay (Hungarian Foreign Minister), written by Sztójay, concluded: "Sooner or later a positive German intervention in the problem of the position of Jewry in Hungary must be expected." [126] Here Sztójay was reiterating remarks he had made in another report still one year earlier, in August 1942.[127] Thus even though the direct orders for round-up and deportation of the Hungarian Jews

---

[125] Bettina Stangneth, *Eichmann Before Jerusalem: The Unexamined Life of a Mass Mu*rderer.Translated from the German by Ruth Martin (New York: Alfred a. Knopf, 2014), Ch.2 and passim.

[126] Levai, *Black Book*, 33.

[127] Ibid., 25.

were sent out by the Hungarian Ministry of the Interior to the
Gendarmerie and police forces throughout the country, the demand
came ultimately from Hitler, through the main German "operatives"
in Hungary, Eichmann, Kaltenbrunner and Veesenmeyer. In July
1944, partly with the aid of international pressure, Horthy was able
to block deportation of the Jews of Budapest. But in October he
was overthrown and replaced, with German assistance and encouragement, by Ferenc Szálasi, leader of the Arrow Cross movement,
the Hungarian equivalent of National Socialists. After the overthrow, efforts at persecution were renewed. We could say that in
Hungary, as in Germany, many members of the government, civil
servants, military and police, and perhaps civilians, had from early
on been "working towards Hitler."[128] That is to say, in Hungary, as
in Germany, there was a process of "cumulative radicalization" of the
bureaucracy and of the population such that when the German invasion provided an opportunity for "de-Jewification" of the country,
the Hungarians ran with it.[129] All the material (economic and territorial) *Realpolitik* considerations can't obscure the deep-seated, quite
traditional, part-religious, part- ethnic antisemitism of Hungarian
officials, such as Ferenczy near the top and others, such as local
mayors (for example, Czoga in Szatmárnémeti) further down the
power ladder. That was not the product of Nazi policy. As in other
countries, it had developed as it were indigenously over centuries.
Hungarian leaders and many in the population -genuine attempts
at rescue and assistance notwithstanding--came to the same racial
views and to the demand for protection of "the purity of. Christian
blood" on their own. The Jews had been a "tolerated" minority

---

[128] This concept was introduced by the historian Ian Kershaw in *Hitler: 1889-
1936: Hubris* (New York: W.W.Norton, 1999), xxix. The idea is that officials,
military personnel and civilians could all work to achieve Hitler's goals without explicit instructions from him. In this way, people became immersed in
a process of increasing radicalization.

[129] Kovács, "Hungarian Intentionalism," 12.

since 1867, but they were perhaps never more than that, despite the deep desire of many Jews to be fully part of the Hungarian or Magyar nation. In the parliamentary debate leading up to passage of the Second [anti]-]Jewish Bill in December 1938, an appeal was submitted by representatives of the Jewish community:

"[There] is no human law that can deprive us of our Hungarian fatherland, even less does there exist a man-made law that can prevent us from worshipping our God. Just as the trials of bygone centuries –whether by fire or water, scaffold, stake, galleys or chains— were unable to confound us in our faith, so we shall stand by our Hungarian country, whose language is our language and whose history is our life (just as our fellow-worshippers retained the use of their Spanish tongue)."[130]

Tragically, the feeling was reciprocated only in a very restricted manner.

Did Transylvania Have a Special Role During the Hitler Era?

This question arises because of new scholarship on the "Transylvanian Question" by Holly Case, and other work on the "borderlands" of Eastern Europe, that is lands between the German and Russian or Soviet states.[131] In all these territories, it is argued, ancient ethnic conflicts strongly modulated post-World War I state-formation processes. Case argues in particular that in the nineteenth and twentieth centuries Transylvania was pivotal in the articulation of new visions for Europe. The ruling classes in both Hungary and Romania regarded the territorial integrity of the region, the protection of the Hungarian minority in the south, and the Romanian minority in the north, as essential to the dignity and greatness of their respective nations. They put this case repeat-

---

[130] Quoted in Levai, *Black Book*, 15.
[131] Cf. Footnotes 3, 27 above.

edly during the nineteenth century, during the Versailles/Trianon negotiations, and to Hitler and Stalin. Case acknowledges that nothing could happen in Transylvania without the acquiescence of the great powers, but heavily emphasizes the autochthonous policies and decisions pursued by Romania and Hungary.

I believe, by contrast, that while the ethnic and national conflicts relating to Transylvania may illuminate ethnic conflict more broadly, as well as particular national agendas at any given moment, the main conclusion to be drawn is that small states *don't* matter in international politics and the shaping of the European vision, if there is such a thing. Relatively small states, like Hungary and Romania, Estonia and Lithuania, mattered during World War II only insofar as they were useful −as sources of oil, of agricultural goods, or as transit zones —to the much larger and more powerful states.

Moreover, in Case's study the history and plight of the Jews of Transylvania, especially during the Hitler era, emerge merely at the intersection of other issues; centuries-old relations with and attitudes toward Jews seem to have virtually no role in the formation of indigenous Hungarian and Romanian fascism. "Policy and practice vis à vis Jews in these states were thus inextricably bound to minority policy more generally, and ultimately to territorial considerations."[132] This is simply not an adequate description of either Hungarian or Romanian attitudes and policies toward the Jewish minorities either in their "core" lands or in their Transylvanian holdings. These attitudes were a longstanding mixture of religious hatred, economic resentment, and social antipathy which "prepared the ground" for when the Germans arrived. The specifically-named anti-Jewish laws in Hungary, passed between 1938 and 1941, were not aimed at other minorities. Even when legislation was passed, for example in Romania, restricting the rights of other minorities, the Jews were usually more severely restricted, certainly in the application of the

---

[132] Case, *Between States*, 186.

rulings and decrees. Although Serbs, Romanians and other "undesirables" were recruited into labor service battalions by Hungary, the
harshest conditions were usually reserved for the Jewish recruits, of
whatever (other) nationality.

Case's insistence on the centrality of the Transylvanian question
not only leads her to see the Holocaust as predominantly colored by
transnational territorial concerns, rather than German aims combined with national, ideological forms of antisemitism. It also leads
her to seriously downplay the other strategic considerations of both
Hungary and Romania in their war-time decision-making.

"Hungarian and Romanian leaders gambled with the fates of
millions…in the interest of resolving the Transylvanian Question
in their favor, betting with the lives of front soldiers, minorities, and
their own presumed ethnic constituencies on the outcome of a future
peace settlement. But by far the most extreme form of this type of
gambling with ideologies and the fates of the region's inhabitants was
the treatment of the Jews…murdered and "saved" all according to
the Hungarian and Romanian states leaders' sense of whether and
how the Jews might figure into the resolution of the Transylvanian
Question."[133]

Neither the Hungarians nor the Romanians were "gambling,"
any more than they had in 1914, or more than any other country
was. Both countries aligned themselves with Germany not only because of Transylvania, though the revision of borders or recuperation
of territories lost through the Trianon Treaty was certainly of vital
importance, as Case and others have demonstrated beyond doubt.
But they also wanted to realize or perpetuate a highly conservative
political and social vision with which they were in basic agreement.
It was a conception, one could call it a cultural code, which relied
heavily on persecution of Jews, Slavs and others, and on the struggle

---

[133] Ibid., 195.

against Soviet communism.[134] A vision for the future of Europe was indeed at stake, but of course no one could foresee the outcome of the struggle. It was a titanic struggle that was not just about proving who "deserved" Transylvania.

Are There Political Lessons from the Holocaust Overall?

The *doyen* of the history of the Holocaust in Hungary, Randolph L. Braham, remarked that the cruelty of the Hungarians in the management of the labor service battalions (into which my father was drafted) was foreshadowed by the cruelty of the counterrevolutionaries in 1919. At that time, in the course of the collapse of the Russian, Austrian, and German empires, and in the wake of the Bolshevik Revolution in Russia in 1917, communist revolutionaries strove mightily to establish new modes of government through workers' councils (soviets) throughout Central and Eastern Europe; as in the case of Russia, this called forth a large and bitter wave of counterrevolutionary violence by remaining monarchist and other conservative forces. Braham's remark may well be correct, but it seems to lead us to taking a look at still earlier periods of revolution and reaction, dating back at least to the French revolution of 1789, if not earlier. One might even say that the philosopher of history G.W.F. Hegel was in a sense right: between 1830 and 1939, throughout Europe and Russia, there was a *dialectic* between uprising and repression, thesis and antithesis, with the forces of harsh conservatism ultimately in the ascendant, even after adopting constitutions and other liberal measures (that is, in Hegelian terms, even when liberal reforms were "sublimated" into the next, reactionary, historical

---

[134] The concept of a cultural code was introduced by the historian Shulamit Volkov in *Antisemitismus als kultureller Code: Zehn Essays* (Munchen: Verlag C.H. Beck,1990).

phase). Writing about the second half of the nineteenth century in France, one historian has written:

"[T]he history of the first four months of the Second Republic is the history of a growing divergence between the moderate republicans, who had the confidence of a majority of the French, and the radical republicans, who had the support of the Paris working class." And: "the results of the [April 1848 election] showed the essentially moderate and even conservative character of the country as a whole as opposed to the radical complexion of the capital. Out of nine-hundred seats, approximately five hundred went to moderate republicans and only one hundred to radicals."[135]

Seen in this light, the revolutions and reactions of 1919, and the subsequent struggles between moderate conservatives, extreme conservatives, and parties and protagonists of the Left in Germany, Austria, Hungary, Russia and other parts of Europe, were part of a much older pattern. Folded into this centuries-old dialectic (as Hegel also maintained) were the imperial conquerors, tyrannical sociopaths and other "world-historical individuals" who permanently shifted the lives of nations: Napoleon, Marx, Lenin, Stalin, and quite a few others. Perhaps the conqueror with imperial ambition, and the tyrannical sociopath, are perennial personality types, though the technology and material forces available to modern conquerors and tyrants is obviously quite different from those of say, Alexander the Great, Charlemagne or Napoleon.

Observing these longstanding patterns, should we adopt Hegel's cold-hearted stance and proclaim that it is futile to indulge in "moral sadness" at the fact that human history has proved to be a "slaughter-bench"? This is impossible for anyone with a modicum of natural compassion, and especially when those slaughtered are one's own family. It is also very difficult if one's own family participated directly in the slaughter or was indirectly responsible for it in some

---

[135] Charles Breunig, *Age of Revolution and Reaction, 1789-1850* (New York: W.W. Norton & Co., 1970), 257, 258.

way.[136] To ignore such family involvement, which affects almost everyone, is a psychological impossibility, unless it arises from a willful and near-total ignorance, or an equally near-total incapacity for reflection. It is in part for this reason that nationalism endures: large collectivities, united either by ethnicity and/or the fact of having been through certain events together, are not often willing to give up the memories of those experiences, even though the events may have taken place centuries ago, and even though their thinking about their collective identity may be partially mistaken or confused. (I am thinking here of Ernest Renan's remark that "the essential element of a nation is that all of its individuals must have many things in common, [but] they must also have forgotten many things.") To strive, as Hegel did, to rise above these existential struggles and summarize them in a general, abstract way as a grand, impersonal, dialectical movement of the world toward freedom does not strike one even as wrong, but simply as irrelevant.

Beyond this dialectic of Left and Right in the nineteenth and twentieth centuries, historians have pinpointed certain critical moments in the downfall of German democracy and the advent of Hitler. I would go somewhat further and maintain that such moments were of a type which continues to repeat itself, and which can be discerned in a variety of contemporary situations. Simply put, these were *undemocratic* moments, even if they were not always straightforwardly unconstitutional ones. Some examples: the use of non-state forces, alongside state forces of law and order, to suppress political unrest or insurrection (Chancellor Gustav Noske during the quelling of the Spartacus Rising, January 1919); wholesale removal of a provincial government by the central government (von Papen removes the Prussian state government, July 1932); dissolution of representative bodies, e.g. a parliament, in order to circumvent or avoid detailed inter-party negotiations (Chancellor Brüning, July 1930);

---

[136] Cf. Geraldine Schwartz, *Those Who Forget* (New York: Scribner, 2020).

"acceptance of a high level of political violence," and "brutalization of society engendered by war and near civil war."[137] To this list we can add: continual, pervasive use of disinformation, propaganda and dehumanizing language in all forms of public media (newspapers, pamphlets, films, speeches, mass rallies). In Austria and Hungary, processes similar to those in Germany also took place, even if there was something of a time-lag and the conservatives were not in complete alignment with the German National Socialists. The conservative governments in those countries, which followed the Nuremberg Laws with their own anti-Jewish measures, eventually gave way to the far-Right Austrian National Socialists and the Hungarian Arrow Cross. As Ian Kershaw sums up: "Without the self-destructiveness of the democratic state, without the wish to undermine democracy of those who were meant to uphold it, Hitler would not have come close to power."[138]

The differences between the relatively moderate conservatives and the far- Right movements and parties corresponds to the distinction between reformist and revolutionary politics. What happened was largely facilitated by the weakness of moderate conservatives in contrast to the single-mindedness of the revolutionaries on both Right and Left. The sheer organizational energy and willpower of Lenin and Trotsky, Hitler and Goebbels, simply was not or could not be stopped by the dilatory, bureaucratic, constitutional methods of their --not unaware—opponents. After years of parliamentary activity and lobbying, the Jews in Hungary and elsewhere, and their traditionally conservative supporters, were left powerless. It is dismaying to read, for example in Erno Munkacsi's memoir *How It Happened*, about the letter-and-report-writing, the endless, quite fruitless, meetings and handwringing to which the Jewish Council

---

[137] Kershaw, *Hitler*, 170 See also Rudiger Barth, Hauke Friederichs, *Die Totengraber: Der letzte Winter der Weimarer Republik* (Frankfurt am Main: Fischer Taschenbuch Verlag, 2019).

[138] Kershaw, *Hitler*, 322.

of Budapest was reduced in March 1944. As if there was anything they could do at that point. It was way, way too late, with Eichmann ensconced in his expropriated villa in Buda, and his Hungarian colleagues helping to prepare for the "de-Jewification" of Hungary. But it had long been too late for the Horthy government as well. Though Horthy managed to delay a German takeover, at the extremely heavy cost of military support for Hitler's war in the Soviet Union, Germany's power, as well as that of the Soviet Union, had loomed over Hungary since at least the early 1930s. The anti-Jewish measures in Hungary, and even earlier in Poland, were not entirely spontaneous; they were forms of "working toward Hitler," symptoms of "cumulative radicalization," as surely as many of the German people's own response. Or, to adapt Norman Naimark's idea, it may be that Hungary before and during the war was engaged in a process of self-Nazification, just as it undertook a degree of "self-Sovietization" after December 1944.[139] Thus individuals and political parties had an impression that they were free to choose, to act, to make laws, but it was not really so. Social scientists speak of "path-dependent" policies: once one decision is made, rationality requires continuing down one path rather than another, and the degrees of freedom are reduced at each step. In the end, most people, even people and groups with some power in Central and Eastern Europe in the late 1930s, were caught up in the gyrations of the truly great powers at any given time. The moderate conservatives in Hungary during the 1930s were fairly constrained by the shadow of the preponderant Hitler regime and its armies; the same was true of their position, and that of the home-grown communists, vis à vis the Soviets in 1945 and after.

---

[139] Norman Naimark, "The Sovietization of Eastern Europe 1944-1952," in: Melvyn P. Leffler and Odd Arne Wested (eds.), *The Cambridge History of the Cold War. Volume I: Origins: 1945-1962* (Cambridge: Cambridge University Press, 2010), 175-187.

On Writing Jewish History

While reflecting on and debating the philosophy of history from the perspective of Western intellectual history is important, there are several questions which are more directly relevant to Jewish history and historiography. Should the Holocaust be treated principally as part of European history or of Jewish history or both?[140] Does the Holocaust confirm the age-old "lachrymose conception of history," according to which it was the Jews' permanent condition "to study and wander, think and persist, learn and suffer"? Or, as Salo Wittmayer Baron argued, should the focus be on the considerable cultural as well as socio-economic accomplishments of the Jews through the ages? How has the modern discipline of history affected Jewish identity?[141] From the outset (however one exactly dates that), Jewish religion and national identity have been imbued with a sense of history. From the passage in *Devarim* (Deuteronomy) which states "my father was a wandering Aramean," through the Exodus and often-repeated divine insistence that Jews recall how they were brought out of Egypt, to the Russian playwright S. Anski's admonition "woe to the people whose history is written by strange hands," historical consciousness and the importance of remembering and recording has been central. By the twentieth century, however, the many results of historical research by both Jews and non-Jews had created what is often called a crisis of historicism.[142] Given the doubts sown about numerous events described in the Bible, and about the actual historical existence of critical figures such as Abraham, could and should the text retain its status as divinely revealed in the tradi-

---

[140] CF. David Engel, *Historians of the Jews and the Holocaust* (Stanford: Stanford University Press,2010).

[141] Cf. Ismar Schorsch, *From Text to Context: The Turn to History in Modern Judaism* (Hanover and London: University Press of New England,1994).

[142] Cf. David N. Myers, *Resisting History: Historicism and Its discontents in German-Jewish Thought* (Princeton: Princeton University Press,2003).

tional way? if not, how was God to be conceived, and the commandments to be understood? Prior to the Second World War, the Jewish philosophers Hermann Cohen and Franz Rosenzweig attempted, in very different ways, to answer such questions. [143] The Shoah has, of course, enormously exacerbated this problem of the relation between history and God. Rosenzweig's argument that the Jewish people are outside of world history has found echoes but, as I shall try to point out, this view comes with some significant costs.

Does the Holocaust Have a Religious Meaning?

Because historically religion has been central to both Jewish nationhood and individual identity, not only the political questions are important, but also how the Shoah is to be understood theologically and religiously. Given the inexpressible suffering which took place, and the scale of it, how can we continue to think of ourselves as bound up in an eternal covenant with a God who is redeeming and merciful, and who rewards virtue and punishes in a proportional if not evidently just manner? In other words, can we retain the traditional theological framework? On this theme, too, a great deal has been written, and it would be impossible to consider here all the positions taken. I will simply comment on a few perspectives offered by three religious thinkers from Transylvania. This seems only fitting, especially as these figures are also prominent in the world of Jewish thought and philosophy more generally.

Before entering into an examination of the work of the Transylvanian thinkers, however, it will be helpful to outline a relevant portion of the traditional Jewish religious framework, namely

---

[143] Ibid. See also Jean Axelrad Cahan, "Returning to Theology: Further Reflections on Franz Rosenzweig,' in Leonard J. Greenspoon (ed.), *Next Year in Jerusalem: Exile and Return in Jewish History* (West Lafayette, IN: Purdue University Press, 2019).

that which concerns divine reward and punishment. Throughout the Hebrew Bible, but especially in the books *Vayyiqra* (Leviticus) and *Devarim* (Deuteronomy), and in the prophetic writings, Jews are adjured to understand that God intervenes in human history from time to time, as He did particularly during and after the Exodus from Egypt. While the reasons or causes for divine intervention are often inscrutable, there is a pattern of reward and punishment: if Jews carry out the commandments of the Torah and are faithful to God, they will be rewarded, materially, politically, and spiritually: there will be material prosperity; peace and security from their enemies; and God will reside with them. "And I will walk among you, and will be your God, and you shall be my people." (*Vayyiqra* 26:12). On the other hand, if they do not follow the teachings of the Torah, they will be punished: "The lord shall send upon thee cursing, confusion and failure, in all that thy settest thy hand to do, until thou art destroyed…because of the wickedness of thy doings, in that thou hast forsaken me." (*Devarim* 28:20) The idea that punishment will follow upon disobedience found its way into the liturgy for festivals, in the *musaf* service, which includes the famous phrase "because of our sins" (*mipnei chateinu).* Later, perhaps in order to adjust for evident contradictions between experience and this teaching, medieval rabbis and philosophers developed the concept of a world-to-come, *olam ha-ba,* beyond the natural world. While foreshadowed, as was the negative counterpart *sheol,* in the Hebrew Bible, it was not emphasized. The world-to-come of the rabbis and philosophers was deemed to exist on its own metaphysical level. There was a considerable variety of opinion on just what was included in this world, but most insisted that it involved revivification of the dead, without the bodily pleasures of eating, drinking and social communication. It was a place for a kind of moral reward which had not been or could not be achieved in the natural world. Or it could be viewed as an intermediate stage between the natural world and the messianic era or the return to the Garden of Eden. One could, as it were, "go either way": either to the world-to-come or to *gehinnom,* a place of infinite unhappiness: "And many of those that sleep in the dust will wake, these to eternal life, and those to ignominy and eternal abhorrence." (Daniel 7:2) I think it would be useful to call the world-to-come an alternate sphere of justice. As we shall see, a notion of an alternative sphere of justice, with its own metaphysical reality, enters in different ways into the thought of at least two of the post-Holocaust thinkers to be considered here.

Yoel Teitelbaum (1887-1979), was head of the Satmar religious movement based in Szatmárnémeti (its origins were briefly described above). After a brief internment in the Kolosvár ghetto, he managed to get on the famous or infamous Kasztner train out of Hungary (June 1944); his journey required a brief "layover" in Bergen-Belsen. He spent about one year in Palestine, and eventually founded one of the largest Hasidic sects living In North America and Israel. Teitelbaum's sayings and writings about the Holocaust have become highly controversial.

It is not clear (to me) whether Teitelbaum's book *Vayoel Moshe* (*And Moses Agreed,* Brooklyn 1961), was primarily an attempt to explain the Holocaust or constituted one element of a wider campaign to oppose Zionism. In either case, the text argues that Zionism was and is the source of most ills that befall the Jews, including especially the Holocaust. Just as the sin of idolatry was the cause of the destruction of the First Temple, and the sin of baseless hatred was the cause of destruction of the Second Temple, so it was the sin of adherence to Zionism which brought on divine punishment in the form of the Shoah.. "There has never been such a total heresy as Zionism." One can see, from Teitelbaum's point of view, the conceptual necessity of finding a sin to serve as a parallel to the sins which had precipitated the two great previous catastrophes, the destruction of the two Temples and Jerusalem: it was necessary in order to remain on the level of purely religious explanation. By contrast, to call attention to the Assyrians' desire to preempt the Egyptians, in the case of the siege of Jerusalem in the eighth century BCE, or to Roman and German imperial drives in later times, for example, would have displaced the discussion to the "merely" political level. Accordingly, and keeping to tradition, Teitelbaum held that in the face of sin the righteous are punished along with the wicked; millions of non-Zionists had to perish along with the adherents of the movement. But in what way was Zionism a sin?

According to Teitelbaum, Zionism is a sin in at least two respects. First, it constitutes a violation of the "three oaths" between God and Israel. These were first adumbrated in the Biblical *Song of Songs*, and later explicated in the Talmudic Tractate *Ketubot*: i) the people Israel would not go up to the land of Israel as a whole or *en masse*, ii) Israel would not rebel against the other nations of the world, and iii) God would provide that the other nations would not oppress Israel. Since the first and second oaths had been broken, by Jews "forcing the end," that is, attempting to bring about the messianic era on their own terms, without divine aid, the third oath could not be upheld. By taking steps to conquer the land of Palestine, and by carrying out military actions, Zionists created the conditions for the Jews' own destruction. But Zionism was also a sin, according to Teitelbaum, insofar as it was founded on atheism. Teitelbaum points to Israel's Declaration of Independence as a glaring example of this, as when it states that "The Land of Israel was the birthplace of the Jewish people. Here their spiritual, religious and political identity was shaped." The error here is that the Declaration fails to acknowledge the Exodus from Egypt and the revelation at Mount Sinai as central to the people's origin.

Although one eminent scholar of ultra-Orthodoxy has suggested that Teitelbaum's text should not be as readily dismissed as it has been outside of Satmar circles, most commentators, whether religious or secular, find it deeply offensive.[144] They rightly ask, how could anyone possibly believe that the brutal murder of six million Jews, including one million children, was part of a divine purpose that is moral and just? Teitelbaum himself seems to anticipate this question to some extent. He states: "Three responses to the argument that since only a few Zionists, mainly in Eretz Yisroel, violated the oaths, why did the entire Jewish people in Europe suffer?" The response:

"1) For an oath, the whole world is punished for the violation of an individual, and certainly for a large percentage.

2) Even among those who did not help the Zionists, most did not protest.

3) Punishment always begins with the righteous."

Teitelbaum gives various examples to support the last claim. I will cite only two: In *parashat nizzavim* (Deuteronomy 29:9- 30:20) we read that God's covenant is "neither with you only" but also "with him that is not here with us today." So that if one person chooses to go and serve the gods of other nations, and to "walk in the stubbornness of [his] heart," not only will divine anger be directed against him, but the whole land will be brimstone, salt and burning .And future generations, wondering what had happened, will learn that "the Lord rooted them out of their land in anger." Similarly, in *Yehoshua* (Joshua) 22:20 we read that Akhan, who stole consecrated

---

[144] See, for example, the exchange between scholars Shaul Magid, James A. Diamond and Menachem Kellner in the pages of the online magazine *Tablet*: Shaul Magid, "The Satmar Are Anti-Zionist: Should We Care?" *Tablet Magazine*, May 20, 2020; James A. Diamond, Menachem Kellner and Shaul Magid, "A Reply to Shaul Magid on Satmar Rebbe Yoel Teitelbaum's Anti-Zioinst Theology," *Tablet Magazine,* June 15, 2020.

goods in Yeriho (Jericho) "perished not alone in his iniquity." Others were punished as well. For Teitelbaum, these instances, as well as the problem of Zionism, underscore a major principle, namely that of co-responsibility. Jews are responsible for one another and should try to stop one another from committing sins. The sin of Zionism is no exception to this, and the implication is that non-Zionists should have tried harder to stop the Zionist movement. Thus Teitelbaum always returns to the same theme: Zionism, even when it was only an intention, a gleam in Herzl's eye, so to speak, was the underlying cause of disaster.

Apart from the objection, mentioned above, which pertains to the nature of God (how could a merciful God allow the murder of the innocent, and on such a scale), there are other fundamental objections to be made to Teitelbaum's point of view, even if one *in principle* accepts the idea of co-responsibility (as many, including liberal Jews, in fact do). A critical one is the actually- existing country of Israel, with its growing population, rich culture and rich agriculture, its scientific achievements, and so on: what should happen now, if we are to follow Teitelbaum's reasoning? The question answers itself: either collective suicide, or war and genocide. I won't pursue that line of thought further.

A more manageable objection comes in the shape of Teitelbaum's distortion of historical evidence. In his version of events, the Jews effectively declared war on Germany, and therefore Germany declared war on them. This particular assertion, outrageous in every respect, occurs in a footnote quoting another of Teitelbaum's works, *Al Hageulah v'al Hatemurah* (*On Redemption and Exchange,* 1967). It draws a direct line between some unspecified Zionist conduct on the one hand and a purported (undated) radio address by Hitler on the other. In this other work Teitelbaum asks:

"But the Zionists do the opposite of the path of Yaakov Avinu: they provoke the nations in a terrible way, recklessly abandoning the blood of Jews. Did they not declare war against the terrible enemy in Germany?... It is impossible to understand how they could be so cruel, knowing that a large percentage of the Jewish people were under his power, and they could nothing about it – how could they be so cruel and abandon Jewish blood?"[145]

It is, rather, impossible to understand how Teitelbaum could conceive that this was an actual sequence of events, that the victims of generations of political and religious violence, of the Nuremberg Laws, and of *Kristallnacht,* were the aggressors, effectively forcing Hitler into his anti-Jewish policies and actions.

There are several consequences to distorting historical events and processes in this way. First, it would tend to make Jews with minimal attachment to tradition run still further away from what they are already tempted to regard as an absurdity. Second, it complicates some theoretical issues as well. For example, if empirically-based historical studies apparently count for nothing, as in the case presented above by Teitelbaum (the Jews attacked their host nation, the Germans, therefore Hitler attacked them), why should anyone accept other facets of Jewish history as real, such as the existence of the First and Second Temples? This problem was introduced long ago, in Maimonides' discussion of which parts of the Hebrew Bible should be interpreted literally and which metaphorically. Spinoza famously responded to Maimonides in his outline of a method of text criticism in the *Theologico-Political Treatise.* He insisted on avoiding metaphorical interpretation as much as possible and relying primarily on rigorously accumulated and analyzed historical evidence. Teitelbaum would not have time for this philosophical exchange between the two great Jewish thinkers, but that doesn't make the conceptual issues any less real. I shall return to this point below.

We might note, however, that another Hungarian representative of Hasidic Judaism, Yissachar Taykhtal (1885-1945) held exactly the opposite view to Teitelbaum's. Taykhtal, born in Nagyhalász,

[145] Cited in [Yoel Teitelbaum], *Introduction to Sefer Vayoel Moshe.* Translated by Rainer Tudid (---)

Transylvania, and connected to the Sanz-Klausenburg dynasty of Hasidic rebbes, wrote in the midst of the Hungarian catastrophe, in 1944. He maintained, in *Eim Habanim Semeichah* (*Happy Mother of Children*), that it was the sin of *opposing* Zionism, and succumbing to assimilation, which had led to disaster. Taykhtal was murdered by a fellow prisoner, a Ukrainian, while on a train from Auschwitz to Mauthausen.

Eliezer Berkovits (1908-1992), like Teitelbaum, was born in Transylvania, in Nagyvárad (Oradea), into an Orthodox family. But taking a somewhat daring step he earned a doctorate in philosophy at the University of Berlin in 1933, and was able to leave the Continent in 1939. After a period in Leeds, England he moved to Sydney, Australia (1946-1950) and ultimately Skokie, Illinois, where he became a revered teacher. His written work was very extensive, dealing a with a great variety of topics. What concerns me here is the question of faith after the Holocaust, which is the title of one of Berkovits's major works, published in 1973.

Berkovits begins *Faith After the Holocaust* with the heartfelt declaration that he understands what he calls "holy disbelief." Even though there were many who entered the gas chambers chanting *"ani ma'amin"* ("I believe," Maimonides' thirteen principles of faith transposed into poetry and sung), anyone who lived through the ghettoes and camps and came to the view that God either does not exist or is not as He was traditionally understood, cannot be blamed for this. Those who were not actually there have no right to remonstrate. Berkovits is acutely aware of the magnitude of the problem. It is not just that God somehow failed to respond (as He had, for example, in Egypt). Rather "the question is whether within the frame of reference of Judaism it is possible to take cognizance of the tragedy and hold on to the promise of existence in spite of the tragedy."[146] For centuries, after disaster struck, Jews had returned to their

---

[146] Eliezer Berkovits, *Faith After the Holocaust* (New York: Ktav Publishing House, 1973), 85.

faith or renewed their commitment with the attitude "nevertheless and in spite of it all." Is that possible in this situation? Berkovits will answer that it is possible, because God was not responsible for the Holocaust, human beings were. Moreover, there are other considerations. His aim, he says, is not to provide a theodicy, a justification of God's ways; he is clear that he does not think that can be done. "The idea that Jewish martyrology through the ages can be explained as divine judgement is obscene.... . What happened to European Jewry in our generation...was injustice absolute, countenanced by God." [147] But he is attempting to indicate an intellectual and spiritual path forward, a way of thinking which will allow a resumption of Jewish religious tradition and the continuation of the people Israel in their specific identity.

The first step is a re-thinking of God's nature. Berkovits shifts the emphasis from God as arranger of miracles and lawgiver to God as a hidden god (*el mistater*). He cites numerous Biblical and other texts that refer to God's silence and absence. Indeed, it is important to distinguish between silence and absence. The conclusion that God was or is *absent* is an entirely different proposition; it indicates not "holy disbelief" but a nihilistic lack of belief altogether. As if to answer Albert Camus, who declared the world absurd, or Rebbe Mendel of Kotsk (1787-1859) who cried out in bewilderment: "Does this palace have a lord?" Berkovits quotes Rabbi Akiva's affirmation: "Still there is judgement and there is a Judge." [148] For Berkovits this means that despite the Holocaust and the apparent silence and hiddenness of God, the world is not without divine governance and without justice, though it may be difficult to discern.

Berkovits acknowledges that the last claim may be unconvincing: "How can one prove an unconvincing presence convincingly?" [149] One piece of evidence, Berkovits believes, is the sheer survival of the

[147] Ibid., 94.
[148] Ibid.,99.
[149] Ibid., 107.

Jewish people (Israel) through thousands of years. The fact that a relatively very small and powerless nation has endured the rise and fall of a multiplicity of empires, kingdoms and rulers is proof of a distinctive historical and religious role. The ideas that this people represents – an aniconic conception of God, with its injunctions against idolatry, and the whole structure of religious and moral laws and teachings – remain in the world, and for Berkovits that cannot be a matter of contingency. "All history advised against it, [but] this fantastic concept became a fact of history." [150]

Indeed, Berkovits sees the perdurance of the Jews and Judaism as taking place on two levels, the natural and the "supra-natural." [151] Both exist within the world, within the same dimension, as he puts it, but they are distinct. Throughout most of (natural) human history, the supra-natural is present but non-intervening; humans are free to make of their world and their lives what they will. "God took a risk with man...."[152] Following this initial step, God is extremely "forbearing." His mercy toward sinners is such that He mostly refrains from intervention, and this "necessitates the abandonment of some men to a fate they may well experience as divine indifference to justice and human suffering."[153] Nonetheless from time to time the two levels of reality intersect, the supra-natural or divine level inserts itself into the natural: "Thus in the naturalistic realm occasionally the Voice is heard, a glimpse is gained of the supra-natural."[154]

Although he had stated that it was not his intention, it seems that Berkovits is indeed offering a justification of God's ways, a theodicy, and is in fact simply reiterating a longstanding philosophical and theological position, the so-called free will defense of traditional theism. But the suffering of six million Jews and many millions of

---

[150] Ibid., 111.
[151] Ibid.
[152] Ibid.107.
[153] Ibid., 106.
[154] Ibid., 111.

others during the last world war was not merely the abandonment of "some men."

Moreover, the idea of two levels of reality is only incompletely stated. The two levels are labelled the axiological and the ontological: the axiological is the sphere of human ethics, in which humans have the opportunity to model themselves after the (anthropomorphic) conception of God with its loving, merciful and just divine personality; the ontological is the sphere of divine being as an abstract philosophical god, who can neither be comprehended nor addressed. "In a sense, God can be neither good nor bad. In terms of His own nature He is incapable of evil. He is the only one who *is* goodness. ...One might also say that with man the good is axiology; with God, ontology ...Man alone can strive and struggle for the good; God *is* good [emphasis mine]."[155] While God's being as perfect goodness may be concealed from us (put traditionally, His face may be hidden), nonetheless the perfection of His being cannot be diminished in any way.

This conception of God's being is not new. What Berkovits seems to have in mind could equally be said of the One of Parmenides, or the ideal of goodness of Hermann Cohen, or the divine substance of Spinoza. Unlike these other philosophers, however, Berkovits does not attempt to provide a persuasive, let alone compelling, explanation as to how the perfectly good, but quite abstract, divine being relates to the "intramundane," that is, to the natural and human worlds. He does not provide any explanation of how the two levels, the axiological and the ontological, are linked. He simply asserts that there is occasionally some sort of encounter between the levels of reality. He adds: "[t]he history of the nations is enacted mainly in the realm of the Is. It is naturalistic history, essentially power history. [But] the history of Israel belongs chiefly in the realm of the Ought [axiology]; it is faith history, faith that what ought to be, what ought to determine and guide human life, should be and will be."[156]

155 Ibid., 104-105.
156 Ibid., 112.

A principal consequence of Berkovits'-- and Teitelbaum's -- view that there is a realm of reality that is transcendent to or at least distinct from the natural world, is that while it *appears* that cruel tyrants and conquerors bestride the world, in an ultimate sense they are nothing, they have no reality. This is a consoling thought, but probably not for someone whose child will imminently be shot or turned to smoke. As Spinoza, who had a similar conception long before Berkovits, wrote, the philosophical god is not a god to whom one can pray.

Another consequence of Berkovits' postulation of (at least) two levels of reality, the natural and the supra-natural, is that it allows him to discuss what he calls "the metaphysics of barbarism,"[157] in other words, antisemitism. In his view, the perdurance of the Jewish people and what they have traditionally stood for, "the staying power of Jewish powerlessness," explains the "metaphysical fear" that other peoples have vis à vis the Jews.[158] The Jews' continued existence threatens the "main preoccupations of power history," and leads other nations to "satanic self-assertion,' in which the God of the Jews is denied or superseded, and the Jewish people attacked and put to death.

I have addressed the topic of metaphysical antisemitism at length elsewhere, and will only repeat my main thesis here.[159] I don't think the notion of metaphysical antisemitism helps to explain the phenomenon, which is not unitary and does not have a single cause. Antisemitism is a *constellation* of tropes and practices, and any given occurrence, including the antisemitism of the Nazi era, must be analyzed in its own time and context. At certain moments what is involved is economic resentment or envy; at other times it is a familiar religious hatred; at still other times, it has been sheer bio-

---

[157] Ibid.,117.

[158] Ibid.,119.

[159] See Jean Axelrad Cahan, "Can Antisemitism have a Sacral Quality? Reflections on Wistrich and Others," *Antisemitism Studies,* 3:1 (April 2019).

logical racism; or it could be a combination of all of these. Religious antisemitism or anti-Judaism has its own logic and ontology, which again depend on the source. Nothing is gained by announcing that an old religious prejudice is metaphysical in nature. While religious ideas can be analyzed using metaphysical concepts, *in themselves* such concepts are neutral, like numbers. They have no power. The claim that antisemitism is metaphysical tries to transfer hatred from the human social world to some exalted conceptual realm, making it difficult to counter or correct. Nor is the *intensity* of religious and ethnic hatreds explained by describing it as metaphysical. This, too, makes antisemitism appear to be beyond the structure of the world and implies that there is nothing to be done about it, except perhaps to write counter- theological and philosophical treatises. If there is to be any improvement in inter-ethnic and international communication, any advancement in human rights, non-violent politics and de-radicalization, we cannot remain in the realm of metaphysics, however much that may illuminate certain religious questions.

Elie Wiesel (1928-2016), from an Orthodox family in Maramossighet, east of Szatmárnémeti in Northern Transylvania, was not ready either to remain totally accepting of traditional religious ideas or to abandon them. "In my opinion, a Jew can rebel against God, on condition that he stay with Him."[160] In other words the Jew can and should hold on to belief in the existence of God, and retain the traditional customs and rituals of Judaism, but should not stop asking questions and should not yield to facile answers. Wiesel constantly reiterated the persistence of the fundamental question: why did God not intervene to bring an end to the suffering during the Shoah? In his memoir *All Rivers Run to the Sea* (1995) he writes:

"Nothing justifies Auschwitz and Treblinka. Were the Lord Himself to offer me a justification, I think I would reject it. ...Faced with unprecedented suffering and agony, he should have intervened,

[160] Wiesel, *All Rivers*, 284.

or at least expressed Himself. …But I find myself equally ignorant as regards men. I will never understand their moral decline…"[161]

Of the three positions sketched here, I find myself closest to that of Wiesel, but I would put the position somewhat differently. Following Emile Durkheim's *Elementary Forms of Religious Life* (1912), I would say that many of the principles, rituals and practices of traditional Judaism, with their sources in the Torah and the Talmud, which cover all aspects of individual and collective life, remain not only beneficial but beautiful in and for everyday life, and central to our collective identity.They remain, as Rabbi Akiva insisted, the Jewish habitat, without which we would not be who we are, even in our diversity. But through the Holocaust the *conceptual* dimension of Judaism has been dangerously damaged, if it has not fully disintegrated. The conceptual foundation, consisting of the Biblical idea of a salvific, personal God, and the binding covenant with Him, is, for many, too difficult to sustain. Even if one takes as foundational the more abstract conceptions of God constructed by philosophers such as Maimonides, after Auschwitz the idea of the covenant still seems irreparably broken. The most psychologically feasible route may therefore be a pragmatic one; that is to say, living in and with Judaism in all its diversity, and not thinking too much about the ultimate foundations.

Numerous thinkers, such Hans Jonas, Arthur Cohen, and Emmanuel Levinas attempted to work out a new philosophical interpretation or understanding of God after the Holocaust. Each of these conceptions is plausible in its own way. But, as mentioned earlier, a philosophical conception is difficult to accept as a substitute for the divine personality of tradition, to whom one could at least occasionally feel close. The religious thinker Irving Greenberg, meanwhile, has argued that if there is to be a covenant with the hidden, silent and seemingly indifferent God, whether Biblical or

---

[161] Wiesel, *All Rivers*, excerpted in Katz, *Wrestling*, 683.

philosophical, it will have to be of a different order than the previous
ones. In his essay "The Third Great Cycle of Jewish History" (1981)
he wrote:

"What then happened to the covenant? I submit that its authority was broken but the Jewish people, released from its obligations,
chose voluntarily to take it on again. We are living in the age of
the renewal of the covenant. God was no longer in a position to
command, but the Jewish people was so in love with the dream of
redemption that it volunteered to carry on the mission. ..."[162]

The renewed covenantal responsibilities for Jews, as Greenberg
sees them, will include rethinking some traditions and practices,
including the treatment of women, attitudes toward non-Jews, political stances within Israel, and so on. But the overall aim should
be to maintain religious commitment in a pluralistic and tolerant
form. It is the religious idea which provides the energy for survival
and renewal of the Jewish people after the latest catastrophe, as in
previous times. In this I am in complete agreement with Greenberg.
For many, however, the feeling will remain that "We received the
Torah at Sinai, and in Lublin we gave it back."[163]

Durkheim thought that the conceptual disintegration of traditional monotheisms had begun either in his own time – the second
half of the nineteenth century-- or perhaps with the Enlightenment.
This is debateable. But again, after the Shoah, the whole structure of
a just and merciful God, in a binding covenant with His "treasure,"
no longer seems tenable. Whether or not science is compatible with
religion, and regardless of other, related questions of modernity, the
sheer scale and quality of the suffering inflicted on the Jews, and
the scale and quality of the pain and effort endured by the soldiers

---

[162] Greenberg, "The Third Great Cycle..." excerpted in Katz (ed.),
Wrestling, 546.
[163] Jacob Glatstein, "Dead Men Don't Praise God," quoted in Katz,
Wrestling, 544.

and civilians of other nations in order to overthrow Hitler and his regime, is just too much for the ancient framework to bear.

"The scope of the catastrophe is so terrible, and our disaster is 'great like the sea,' that it cannot be absorbed by our ideas..... It is impossible to encircle the mourning entirely, because it is greater than our intellect's grasp and deeper than our normal feelings. Therefore each of us must contract ourselves into our own corner, each to his own mourning."[164]

Exodus Politics?

But, one might still counter to all of the above, in the end there *were* some who survived the Holocaust, and as in the past they represent a "holy remnant," a fraction of the Jewish people whom God had allowed to survive a catastrophe, such as war or the destruction of the Temple, or to exit their condition of slavery, as in the original Exodus. It then became their special obligation to live out Jewish values and principles. Is the idea of a holy remnant, and a comparison with the Biblical Exodus, viable or helpful after the Shoah?

The distinguished political philosopher Michael Walzer argued, in *Exodus and Revolution* (1985), that the original Exodus was the result of both human leadership and choice (he leaves open or unaddressed the question of divine power). It was a *decision*: "The Exodus is not a lucky escape from misfortune. Rather, the misfortune has a moral character, and the escape a world-historical meaning. Egypt is not just left behind, it is rejected."[165] And, in Walzer's account, it led to a gradual, if grumbling, commitment to seek ever more just distributions of power and other goods. Thus the Biblical story

---

[164] Yehezkel Sarna, "Toward Penitent Return and Restoration: Words Said…in the Hevron-Knesset Yisroel Yeshiva on 4 December 1944," in Katz, *Wrestling*,137.

[165] Michael Walzer, *Exodus and Revolution* (New York: Basic Books, 1985), 21.

of the Exodus came to be a model for later political movements and traditions. After the Exodus from the condition of slavery in Egypt, and lengthy subsequent wanderings in the desert, the ancient Hebrews committed themselves to a set of laws, and a new political project, as it were. They marched together toward the promised land, literally in a geographic sense, but also socially and politically, toward a more definite form of freedom. Exodus politics is democratic, mostly non-violent (though there were significant deviations from this), and dedicated to social and political reform. It is a type of politics which is not apocalyptic in attitude or messianic in ambition. It is revolutionary only in contrast to the oppression (in the original case, in Egypt) which preceded it; it is not revolutionary in the absolutist, uncompromising mode of modern revolutionaries. (Apart from the seventeenth- century Puritans, Walzer does not name such revolutionaries, but we can assume he means the Jacobins, the Nazis and the Bolsheviks, at least. He does, however, explicitly include the Revisionist movement in pre-state Israel.) As noted above, Walzer emphasizes that the Exodus was not a "lucky escape" from misfortune: for him, the enslavement in Egypt was never inescapable, there were always other possibilities; eventually, through the leadership of Moses, one such possibility was realized.[166]

I find this an unconvincing view of slavery on the one hand, and escape from misfortune on the other. The slavery endured by the Jews in Egypt was reported to have lasted several hundred years; even acknowledging that it is extremely difficult for oppressed, underfed, uneducated people to come to some sort of group or class consciousness of the injustice of their situation, this seems an excessively long time to put up with what is not only a physically extremely debilitating but also an essentially immoral condition. A parallel may be seen, of course, in the history of the enslavement of Africans in the Americas and the Caribbean. The problem, and

---

[166] Ibid.

the answer, is that, despite our liberal and democratic fantasies, there are *not* always alternatives and opportunities for deliverance or liberation, because of inequalities of sheer physical and military strength, and forms of social and political power which rest on these. That was the underlying obstacle to greater resistance by Jews during the Holocaust. And what the repeated failures of Russian reformers as well as revolutionaries in the nineteenth century; the Europe-wide failures of liberal reforms in 1848; the eventual success of the Leninist Bolsheviks and the seizure of power by Hitler and the Nazis (who in 1932 had a paramilitary force of 450,000 men, compared to the state's 100,000 permitted by the Versailles Treaty) show is surely that relatively moderate "Exodus politics," with a vision of greater justice, often doesn't work. It strikes me, therefore, both as a highly desirable form of politics, and yet doomed to frequent and profound defeats.

An alternative model (to the original Exodus) for thinking about the remnant that survived the Holocaust and its potential opportunities and responsibilities, one to which Walzer himself points, might be that of the Ezra-Nehemiah story. After the catastrophe of the destruction of the First Temple in Jerusalem (586 BCE), and exile in Babylon, Ezra, Nehemiah and a small additional group persuade King Cyrus of Persia to let them return to Jerusalem to restore the Temple. He generously agrees, and, after considerable difficulty, they succeed. But unlike Walzer, I do not see this as a case of a second Exodus. This story was about a *choice* to *recommit* to the God of the Hebrews and the laws of the Torah, made under more favorable circumstances. It was a choice in a way that the first Exodus was not a choice. The slaves in Egypt were likely barely at subsistence level and had little time to think. The captives in Babylon appear to have been slightly better off; they were subject to a ruler with some degree of empathy, they could consider their options. This could hardly be said of conditions under the adamantine Egyptian pharaoh, let alone Hitler. Moreover, the Exodus from Egypt, though it involved a decision to follow Moses (and the perceived voice of God), ultimately did not come about through the agency of the Hebrews themselves alone. The conditions which permitted it were, apart from the leadership, a set of natural disasters and a military failure, whether one wants to see these as ultimately inflicted by God or not. The liberation from enslavement under Hitler (of course, the six million dead were not liberated in any political sense) was also not a choice on the part of the Jews; it was a byproduct of other peoples' choices, and their supreme physical as well as moral combat (again, whether or not one sees these as ultimately deriving from or directed by God). Moreover, as my parents' postwar experiences in Budapest showed, in some places the liberation was not thought of as a commitment to the freedom promised by a new political order. On the contrary, it was seen by many under Soviet, as opposed to Western, rule as a new type of oppression. There were big differences in patterns of liberation, depending on which of the Allies was carrying it out. Prisoners freed by the Western allies went on, after a transition period, to live in democratic states; those, like my parents, freed or living in zones governed by the Soviets, went on to face another totalitarian society and its political and moral limitations. Neither reform nor revolution was possible in this part of the world for decades.[167]

It is tempting to overlook the sheer physicality of enslavement in any of these cases. And the thought of a purposeful and redemptive ending is very appealing. Yet thinking back to the conditions at Gunskirchen discovered by American troops, one wonders how the survivors could ever transcend the mud and slime, the ashes, the absolute hunger, thirst and disease. These facts must always remain the ground for suspicion of vaulting ambitions in philosophy and theology. But as my parents lives, and especially my father's, indicate, one could also say that survival in Gunskirchen, Auschwitz and

---

[167] There were strong but unsuccessful attempts at overthrow of the existing regimes in East Germany in 1953, Hungary in 1956 and in Poland and Czechoslovakia (1968).

the other death camps was like the emergence of life itself out of a primordial soup. As such it was more than merely physical and was perhaps a sign that, as the rabbis said, the invisible is greater than the visible. That is, there is more that we don't understand than there is of what we do understand. This is a proposition with which even a scientist might agree.

Johannes Axelrad and Hermine Axelrad (née Weissman),
my father's parents. Date unknown.

Rozsi and Samu Fekete with their older daughter Zsusza
and an unidentified friend in Szatmár, 1928.

Zsuzsa (my mother's sister), her husband Zoltan and their little son Jani boating in happier times, probably 1941, before Zoltan was recruited to a labor battalion.

The two former inhabitants (my parents) of Nazi death camps in Genoa, Italy in 1949, en route to Australia.

My father (left) with his parents, sister Emmy, and brother-in-law Feri Mandel (far right) in September 1942. Given the date and partial uniforms of the two young men, this was probably taken during a visit by the family to the two (young men) who had been recruited into labor battalions attached to the Second Hungarian Army in spring 1942.

The crane designed by my father while Chief Engineer at the Obuda Shipyards near Budapest in 1945-47. The crane was used in reconstruction of the renowned Chain Bridge, still a vital feature of Budapest today.

My mother and her first husband, Pal-Janos Adonyi, in Budapest in 1941 or 1942. Pal-Janos, a lawyer, died in a labor-battalion in Ukraine in March 1943.

Rosza Reiter and Samuel (Samu) Fekete at the time of their engagement, about 1910.

My grandfather Samuel Fekete as a medical officer in the Hungarian Army, 1915.

About the Author

Jean Axelrad Cahan was born in Sydney, Australia and grew up in Montreal, Canada. She studied German history at McGill University in Montreal, and received her doctorate in philosophy from Johns Hopkins University in Baltimore, Maryland. She has taught European philosophy at the University of Nebraska-Lincoln for three decades, and helped found the Jewish Studies program there in 1992.

Printed in the United States
by Baker & Taylor Publisher Services